favorite
brand name recipes
C O O K B O O K

Publications International, Ltd.

Pictured on the front cover *(left to right):* Maple-Glazed Cornish Hens *(page 136)*, Spinach Quiche *(page 22)*, Grilled Bruschetta *(page 34)* and Double Chocolate Chip Mini Cheesecakes *(page 234)*.

Pictured on the back cover *(top to bottom):* Hoppin' John *(page 168)*, Pineapple Teriyaki Chicken Kabobs *(page 134)* and Philadelphia® Chocolate-Vanilla Swirl Cheesecake *(page 240)*.

ISBN-13: 978-1-4508-2271-8
ISBN-10: 1-4508-2271-1

Library of Congress Control Number: 2011923514

Manufactured in China.

8 7 6 5 4 3 2 1

Microwave Cooking: Microwave ovens vary in wattage. Use the cooking times as guidelines and check for doneness before adding more time.

Preparation/Cooking Times: Preparation times are based on the approximate amount of time required to assemble the recipe before cooking, baking, chilling or serving. These times include preparation steps such as measuring, chopping and mixing. The fact that some preparations and cooking can be done simultaneously is taken into account. Preparation of optional ingredients and serving suggestions is not included.

Publications International, Ltd.

table
of contents

breakfast & brunch

stuffed french toast with fresh berry topping

2 cups mixed fresh berries (strawberries, raspberries, blueberries and/or blackberries)

2 tablespoons granulated sugar

⅔ cup lowfat ricotta cheese

¼ cup strawberry preserves

3 large eggs

⅔ cup (5 fluid-ounce can) NESTLÉ® CARNATION® Fat Free Evaporated Milk

2 tablespoons packed brown sugar

2 teaspoons vanilla extract

12 slices (about ¾-inch-thick) French bread

1 tablespoon vegetable oil, butter or margarine

Powdered sugar (optional)

Maple syrup, heated (optional)

COMBINE berries and granulated sugar in small bowl. Combine ricotta cheese and strawberry preserves in another small bowl; mix well. Combine eggs, evaporated milk, brown sugar and vanilla extract in pie plate or shallow bowl; mix well.

SPREAD ricotta-preserves mixture evenly over 6 *slices* of bread. Top with *remaining* slices of bread to form sandwiches.

HEAT vegetable oil or butter in large nonstick skillet or griddle over medium heat. Dip sandwiches in egg mixture, coating both sides. Cook on each side for about 2 minutes or until golden brown.

SPRINKLE with powdered sugar; top with berries. Serve with maple syrup, if desired.

Makes 6 servings

skillet sausage with potatoes and rosemary

1 tablespoon vegetable oil	½ teaspoon dried rosemary
3 cups diced red skin potatoes	¼ teaspoon rubbed sage
1 cup diced onion	Salt and black pepper to taste
1 pound BOB EVANS® Original Recipe Roll Sausage	2 tablespoons chopped fresh parsley

Heat oil in large skillet over medium-high heat 1 minute. Add potatoes; cook 5 to 10 minutes or until slightly brown, stirring occasionally. Add onion; cook until tender. Add crumbled sausage; cook until browned. Add rosemary, sage, salt and pepper; cook and stir until well blended. Transfer to serving platter and garnish with parsley. Refrigerate leftovers. *Makes 4 to 6 servings*

caramelized onion & mushroom frittata

¼ cup I CAN'T BELIEVE IT'S NOT BUTTER!® Spread	½ teaspoon chopped fresh thyme leaves OR ⅛ teaspoon dried thyme leaves, crushed
1 medium onion, thinly sliced	⅓ cup shredded Swiss or sharp Cheddar cheese (about 2 ounces)
2 cups sliced mushrooms	
4 eggs, slightly beaten	

Melt I Can't Believe It's Not Butter!® Spread in 10-inch nonstick skillet with ovenproof handle* over medium-high heat and cook onion, stirring occasionally, 5 minutes or until tender. Add mushrooms and cook, stirring occasionally, 4 minutes or until mushrooms are golden. Reduce heat to low and stir in eggs and thyme. Lift set edges of frittata with spatula, tilting pan to allow uncooked mixture to flow to bottom. Cook until almost set. Top with cheese, then broil 2 minutes or until golden brown and eggs are set. *Makes 4 servings*

*To make handle ovenproof, wrap with heavy-duty aluminum foil.

Tip: Substitute 1 cup egg substitute for the eggs.

Prep Time: 15 minutes
Cook Time: 15 minutes

fruit 'n juice breakfast shake

1 extra-ripe, medium DOLE®
Banana

¾ cup DOLE® Pineapple Juice

½ cup lowfat vanilla yogurt

½ cup DOLE® Frozen
Blueberries

COMBINE all ingredients in blender. Blend until smooth.   *Makes 2 servings*

tropical granola

3½ cups QUAKER® Oats (quick
or old fashioned, uncooked)

⅓ cup coarsely chopped slivered
almonds

2 tablespoons finely chopped
crystallized ginger (optional)

½ cup honey

¼ cup (½ stick) butter or
margarine, melted

1½ to 2 teaspoons ground ginger

¼ teaspoon salt

¾ cup chopped dried tropical
fruit mix

1. Heat oven to 350°F.

2. Combine oats, almonds and crystallized ginger, if desired, in large bowl; mix well. Combine honey, butter, ground ginger and salt in small bowl; blend well. Drizzle over oat mixture; mix well. Spread evenly in 15×10-inch jelly-roll pan.

3. Bake 18 to 20 minutes, stirring every 5 minutes. Remove from oven; immediately stir in dried fruit. Cool completely in pan on wire rack. Store in tightly covered container.

Makes 4½ cups

Serving Suggestions: 1) Serve with milk as a breakfast cereal. 2) Layer with low-fat yogurt as a breakfast parfait. 3) Stir into low-fat yogurt for a quick snack. 4) Sprinkle over fresh fruit, ice cream or frozen yogurt for a flavorful dessert.

fruit 'n juice breakfast shake

cinnamon walnut coffee cake

¾ cup chopped walnuts
1 teaspoon ground cinnamon
1¼ cups sugar
1 cup (2 sticks) butter, softened
2 eggs
1 cup sour cream

1⅓ cups all-purpose flour
⅓ cup **CREAM OF WHEAT**®
Cinnamon Swirl Instant
Hot Cereal, uncooked
1½ teaspoons baking powder
½ teaspoon baking soda
1 teaspoon vanilla extract

1. Coat Bundt® pan with nonstick cooking spray. Sprinkle lightly with flour; shake out any excess. Combine walnuts and cinnamon in small bowl; set aside.

2. Cream sugar, butter and eggs in mixing bowl with electric mixer at medium speed. Add sour cream; blend well. Add flour, Cream of Wheat, baking powder and baking soda; mix well. Stir in vanilla. Sprinkle half of walnut mixture into bottom of prepared Bundt pan. Evenly spread half of batter over mixture. Sprinkle remaining walnut mixture over batter. Top with remaining batter, spreading evenly in Bundt pan.

3. Set oven to 350°F (do not preheat); place Bundt pan in cold oven. Bake 45 minutes, or until toothpick inserted into center comes out clean. Remove from oven; let stand 5 minutes. Place serving plate over Bundt pan and turn pan over carefully onto plate; remove pan. Serve cake warm or cool.   *Makes 12 to 16 servings*

Tip: If you do not have a Bundt® pan, you can bake this cake in regular square or round cake pans. Divide the batter between two 8- or 9-inch pans, and sprinkle each with one half of walnut mixture. Bake 25 to 30 minutes.

Prep Time: 15 minutes
Start to Finish Time: 1 hour

bloody marys

1 quart tomato juice
½ cup vodka
2 tablespoons **FRANK'S**®
REDHOT® Original
Cayenne Pepper Sauce

2 tablespoons **FRENCH'S**®
Worcestershire Sauce
2 tablespoons prepared
horseradish
1 tablespoon lemon juice
1 teaspoon celery salt

Combine all ingredients in large pitcher; refrigerate. Serve over ice.

Makes 4 servings

cinnamon walnut coffee cake

tortilla scramble with salsa

8 eggs

¼ cup whipping cream or half-and-half

1 tablespoon butter

3 tablespoons ORTEGA® Salsa, any variety

1 cup broken ORTEGA® Taco Shells

½ cup (2 ounces) shredded Cheddar cheese

Suggested Toppings

Tortilla chips, chopped parsley, ORTEGA® Salsa

Combine eggs and whipping cream in mixing bowl. Beat with wire whisk.

Melt butter in heavy skillet. Add egg mixture and stir in 3 tablespoons salsa. Scramble eggs until they begin to set. Add broken taco shells and cheese, stirring to mix.

Divide egg mixture evenly among individual plates.

Top with tortilla chips, parsley and salsa, if desired.

Makes 4 servings

Prep Time: 5 minutes
Start to Finish Time: 10 minutes

garden veggie hash browns

3 tablespoons vegetable oil

⅓ cup chopped red onion

1 medium zucchini, coarsely chopped

8 stalks asparagus, cut into 1½-inch pieces

½ cup chopped red bell pepper

1½ cups small broccoli florets

1 package SIMPLY POTATOES® Southwest Style Hash Browns

¼ teaspoon salt

¼ teaspoon garlic powder

1. Heat 1 tablespoon oil in 12-inch nonstick skillet. Add onion. Cook over medium heat, stirring occasionally, 2 to 3 minutes. Add zucchini, asparagus, red bell pepper and broccoli. Continue cooking 2 minutes, stirring occasionally, until vegetables are crisp-tender.

2. Add 1 tablespoon oil and Simply Potatoes® to skillet. Spread Simply Potatoes® and vegetables in an even layer; press down lightly with spatula. Sprinkle with salt and garlic powder. Cook 6 to 7 minutes or until golden brown on the bottom. Drizzle with remaining 1 tablespoon oil. Turn Simply Potatoes® over with spatula. Continue cooking 6 to 8 minutes or until golden brown and tender, turning again if necessary.

Makes 6 servings

tortilla scramble with salsa

mixed berry strata

Vegetable cooking spray
5 slices **PEPPERIDGE FARM**® Toasting White Bread, cut into 1-inch pieces
4 eggs
1 cup milk
¼ cup orange juice

½ cup ricotta cheese
¼ cup sugar
2 tablespoons butter, melted
1 bag (12 ounces) frozen mixed berries (strawberries, blueberries, raspberries), thawed and drained
Confectioners' sugar (optional)

1. Spray a 2-quart shallow baking dish with the cooking spray. Place the bread pieces in the dish.

2. Beat the eggs, milk, orange juice, cheese, sugar and butter in a medium bowl with a fork or whisk. Stir in the berries. Pour the egg mixture over the bread pieces. Cover and refrigerate for 2 hours or overnight.

3. Heat the oven to 350°F. Uncover the baking dish.

4. Bake for 40 minutes or until a knife inserted in the center comes out clean. Sprinkle with the confectioners' sugar, if desired.

Makes 4 servings

touchdown cheese scones

2 cups all-purpose flour
2½ teaspoons baking powder
½ teaspoon baking soda
¼ teaspoon salt
2 tablespoons cold butter or margarine, cut in pieces

1 cup shredded mild Cheddar cheese
⅔ cup buttermilk
2 large eggs
½ teaspoon Original **TABASCO**® brand Pepper Sauce

Preheat oven to 350°F. Sift together flour, baking powder, baking soda and salt in large bowl. Cut in butter until mixture resembles cornmeal. Stir in cheese. Blend buttermilk, 1 egg and TABASCO® Sauce together in small bowl. Make a well in center of dry ingredients; add buttermilk mixture. Stir quickly and lightly with fork to form sticky dough. Turn dough out on lightly floured board. Knead gently 10 times. Divide dough in half; pat each half into circle about ½ inch thick. Cut each circle into 4 wedges. Combine remaining egg and 1 tablespoon water. Brush each wedge with egg mixture. Arrange on greased baking sheet. Bake 13 to 15 minutes or until golden.

Makes 8 scones

mixed berry strata

hawaiian breakfast wrap

6 eggs
¼ cup milk OR water
¼ cup chopped ham or Canadian bacon
¼ cup chopped red or green bell pepper

2 tablespoons butter or margarine
1 can (8 ounces) DOLE® Crushed Pineapple, drained
4 (8-inch) flour tortillas

BEAT together eggs and milk in medium bowl until blended. Set aside.

COOK ham and bell pepper in hot butter over medium heat in large nonstick skillet until ham is lightly browned and pepper is tender-crisp. Stir in egg mixture and crushed pineapple. Scramble until desired doneness, stirring constantly.

DIVIDE egg mixture between flour tortillas. Roll sides up. Serve with watermelon wedges and lime slice, if desired. *Makes 4 servings*

Variation: Place mixture on toasted English muffins to serve as a sandwich.

Prep Time: 15 minutes

broccoli, potato & bacon egg pie with cheddar cheese

2 cups cooked broccoli florets
1½ cups cooked diced potatoes (about 2 medium)
1½ cups (lightly packed) grated CABOT® Sharp Cheddar Cheese (about 6 ounces)
4 slices cooked bacon, chopped
1 unbaked 9-inch deep-dish or 10-inch pie shell

6 large eggs
2 large egg yolks
1½ cups heavy cream
1 teaspoon mild paprika
½ teaspoon salt
¼ teaspoon freshly ground black pepper

1. Preheat oven to 350°F.

2. Distribute broccoli, potatoes, cheese and bacon evenly in pie shell. In mixing bowl, whisk together whole eggs and egg yolks until well combined; add cream, paprika, salt and pepper and whisk again.

3. Pour cream mixture evenly over ingredients in pie shell. Bake for 30 to 40 minutes, or until golden on top and set all the way to center. *Makes 6 to 8 servings*

toll house® mini morsel pancakes

2½ cups all-purpose flour
1 cup (6 ounces) NESTLÉ®
   TOLL HOUSE®
   Semi-Sweet Chocolate
   Mini Morsels
1 tablespoon baking powder
½ teaspoon salt
1¾ cups milk

2 large eggs
⅓ cup vegetable oil
⅓ cup packed brown sugar
  Powdered sugar
  Fresh sliced strawberries
   (optional)
  Maple syrup

COMBINE flour, morsels, baking powder and salt in large bowl. Combine milk, eggs, vegetable oil and brown sugar in medium bowl; add to flour mixture. Stir just until moistened (batter may be lumpy).

HEAT griddle or skillet over medium heat; brush lightly with vegetable oil. Pour ¼ *cup* of batter onto hot griddle; cook until bubbles begin to burst. Turn; continue to cook for about 1 minute longer or until golden. Repeat with *remaining* batter.

SPRINKLE with powdered sugar; top with strawberries. Serve with maple syrup.

Makes about 18 pancakes

turkey bacon biscuits

1 (8-ounce) package cream
   cheese, softened
2 eggs
2 tablespoons milk
½ cup shredded Swiss cheese
2 tablespoons chopped green
   onion

1 (10-ounce) can refrigerated
   flaky biscuits
5 JENNIE-O TURKEY
   STORE® Turkey Bacon
   slices, cooked, crumbled,
   divided

Heat oven to 375°F. Grease 10 muffin cups. In small bowl, beat cream cheese, eggs and milk with electric mixer at low speed until smooth. Stir in Swiss cheese and green onion. Separate dough into 10 biscuits. Place 1 biscuit in each greased muffin cup; firmly press in bottom and up sides, forming ¼-inch rim. Place half of bacon in bottom of dough-lined muffin cups. Spoon cheese mixture over bacon. Bake 20 to 25 minutes or until filling is set and biscuits are golden brown. Sprinkle each cup with remaining bacon; lightly press into filling. Remove from pan.

Makes 10 servings

Prep Time: 30 minutes
Cook Time: 30 minutes

cheese strata

6 slices **PEPPERIDGE FARM**® Toasting White Bread, cut into cubes (about 3 cups)

1 can (10¾ ounces) **CAMPBELL'S**® Condensed Cheddar Cheese Soup

1 cup milk

4 eggs

1½ cups shredded Swiss cheese (about 6 ounces)

1. Place the bread cubes into a greased 2-quart shallow baking dish. Beat the soup, milk, eggs and cheese in a medium bowl with a fork or whisk. Pour the milk mixture over the bread cubes. Stir and press the bread cubes into the milk mixture to coat. Cover and refrigerate for 4 hours or overnight. Uncover the baking dish.

2. Bake at 350°F. for 45 minutes or until a knife inserted in the center comes out clean.

Makes 6 servings

Kitchen Tip: This recipe may be doubled to make 12 servings. Double all the ingredients. Divide the ingredients between 2 (2-quart) shallow baking dishes.

breakfast veg•all® burritos

1 tablespoon olive oil

6 ounces cooked chorizo sausage, thinly sliced

1 cup chopped green onions

1 can (15 ounces) **VEG•ALL**® Original Mixed Vegetables, drained

12 eggs, beaten

⅛ teaspoon salt

Pinch black pepper

4 ounces medium Cheddar cheese, shredded

6 (10-inch) flour tortillas

Heat oil in large, heavy-bottomed skillet. Add sausage and green onions and stir until onions are limp and sausage has begun to brown. Add Veg•All and stir for 1 minute, then add beaten eggs, salt and pepper. Stir briskly to scramble eggs. When eggs have begun to set, add cheese.

When eggs are firm, divide them among the 6 tortillas. Fold them into burritos, and serve hot.

Makes 6 servings

Note: This makes six large burritos. To serve smaller appetites, use 6- or 8-inch tortillas and portion out the filling accordingly.

cheese strata

spinach quiche

1 tablespoon vegetable oil

½ onion, chopped

2 tablespoons POLANER® Chopped Garlic

1 bunch spinach, washed, trimmed, chopped*

4 large eggs

½ cup milk

⅓ cup CREAM OF WHEAT® Hot Cereal (Instant, 1-minute, 2½-minute or 10-minute cook time), uncooked

½ teaspoon salt

½ teaspoon ground black pepper

1½ cups shredded sharp Cheddar, colby or Monterey Jack cheese

Or substitute 1 (10-ounce) package frozen chopped spinach, thawed, squeezed dry.

1. Preheat oven to 375°F. Coat 10-inch pie pan with nonstick cooking spray.

2. Heat oil in large skillet over medium-high heat. Add onion and garlic; cook and stir 8 minutes or until soft. Add spinach. Cook and stir until spinach is wilted (if using frozen spinach, cook until heated through). Remove from heat and let cool slightly.

3. Combine eggs, milk, Cream of Wheat, salt and pepper in large bowl; mix well. Stir in spinach mixture and cheese. Pour into prepared pan. Bake 30 minutes or until just firm in center and lightly browned along the edges. Cool 10 minutes before serving.

Makes 6 servings

Tip: Because you don't need a crust for this quick-to-fix, tasty egg-and-cheese pie, you can use this recipe as a starting point for other types of quiche. Substitute any greens for the spinach, and use almost any combination of cheeses for a different flavor. For extra flair, stir in chopped fresh herbs. The quiche is best hot out of the oven, but can be served cold or at room temperature.

Prep Time: 15 minutes
Start to Finish Time: 55 minutes

pineapple orange walnut bread

2 cups all-purpose flour	1 tablespoon grated orange peel
1 teaspoon baking powder	¼ cup orange juice
½ teaspoon baking soda	1 can (8 ounces) DOLE® Crushed Pineapple, undrained
¼ teaspoon salt	
¾ cup sugar	1 cup DOLE® Seedless or Golden Raisins
¼ cup butter or margarine, softened	
1 egg	1 cup chopped walnuts, toasted

COMBINE flour, baking powder, baking soda and salt in medium bowl; set aside.

BEAT together sugar and butter in large bowl until light and fluffy. Beat in egg, orange peel and orange juice. Alternately stir in one third flour mixture and one half undrained crushed pineapple until just blended, ending with flour. Stir in raisins and walnuts.

POUR batter into 9×5-inch loaf pan sprayed with nonstick vegetable cooking spray.

BAKE at 350°F 60 minutes or until toothpick inserted in center comes out clean. Cool in pan 10 minutes; remove from pan and cool completely on wire rack.

Makes 12 servings

Prep Time: 20 minutes
Bake Time: 60 minutes

brunch sandwiches

4 English muffins, split, lightly toasted	8 eggs, fried or poached
8 thin slices CURE 81® ham	8 slices SARGENTO® Deli Style Sliced Swiss Cheese
8 teaspoons Dijon mustard	

1. Top each muffin half with a slice of ham, folding to fit. Spread mustard lightly over ham; top with an egg and one slice cheese.

2. Transfer to foil-lined baking sheet. Broil 4 to 5 inches from heat source until cheese is melted and sandwiches are hot, 2 to 3 minutes.

Makes 4 servings

Prep Time: 5 minutes
Cook Time: 10 minutes

pineapple orange walnut bread

hearty banana oat flapjacks

2 large ripe bananas, peeled
and sliced

1 tablespoon granulated sugar

1 cup all-purpose flour

½ cup QUAKER® Oats (quick
or old fashioned, uncooked)

1 tablespoon baking powder

¼ teaspoon ground cinnamon

¼ teaspoon salt (optional)

1 cup fat-free (skim) milk

1 egg, lightly beaten

2 tablespoons vegetable oil

AUNT JEMIMA® Syrup,
warmed

Additional banana slices
(optional)

Coarsely chopped pecans or
walnuts (optional)

1. Combine banana slices and sugar in medium bowl; stir to coat slices with sugar.
Set aside.

2. Combine flour, oats, baking powder, cinnamon and salt, if desired, in large
bowl; mix well. Combine milk, egg and oil in medium bowl; blend well. Add to dry
ingredients all at once; stir just until dry ingredients are moistened. (Do not overmix.)

3. Heat griddle over medium-high heat (or preheat electric skillet or griddle to 375°F).
Lightly grease griddle. For each pancake, pour scant ¼ cup batter onto hot griddle. Top
with four or five sugar-coated banana slices. Turn pancakes when tops are covered with
bubbles and edges look cooked.

4. Serve with warm syrup and additional banana slices and nuts, if desired.

Makes 12 (4-inch) pancakes

down-home sausage gravy

1 package (16 ounces) fresh
breakfast sausage

2 tablespoons finely chopped
onion

6 tablespoons all-purpose flour

2 cans (12 fluid ounces *each*)
NESTLÉ® CARNATION®
Evaporated Milk

1 cup water

¼ teaspoon salt

Hot pepper sauce to taste

Hot biscuits

COMBINE sausage and onion in large skillet. Cook over medium-low heat, stirring
occasionally, until sausage is no longer pink. Stir in flour; mix well. Stir in evaporated
milk, water, salt and hot pepper sauce. Cook, stirring occasionally, until mixture comes
to a boil. Cook for 1 to 2 minutes.

SERVE immediately over biscuits.

Makes 8 to 10 servings

hearty banana oat flapjacks

appetizers & snacks

original buffalo chicken wings

Zesty Blue Cheese Dip
(page 30)
2½ pounds chicken wings, split
and tips discarded

½ cup FRANK'S® REDHOT®
Original Cayenne Pepper
Sauce (or to taste)
⅓ cup butter or margarine,
melted
Celery sticks

1. Prepare Zesty Blue Cheese Dip.

2. Deep fry* wings at 400°F 12 minutes or until crisp and no longer pink; drain.

3. Combine Frank's RedHot Sauce and butter in large bowl. Add wings to sauce;
toss well to coat evenly. Serve with Zesty Blue Cheese Dip and celery.

Makes 24 to 30 individual pieces

Or prepare wings using one of the cooking methods below. Add wings to sauce; toss well to coat evenly.

To Bake: Place wings in single layer on rack in foil-lined roasting pan. Bake at 425°F
1 hour or until crisp and no longer pink, turning once halfway through baking time.

To Broil: Place wings in single layer on rack in foil-lined roasting pan. Broil 6 inches
from heat 15 to 20 minutes or until crisp and no longer pink, turning once halfway
through cooking time.

To Grill: Place wings on oiled grid. Grill over medium heat 30 to 40 minutes or until
crisp and no longer pink, turning often.

Prep Time: 10 minutes
Cook Time: 15 minutes

continued on page 30

original buffalo chicken wings, continued

zesty blue cheese dip

½ cup blue cheese salad dressing
¼ cup sour cream

2 teaspoons FRANK'S®
REDHOT® Original
Cayenne Pepper Sauce

Combine all ingredients in medium serving bowl; mix well. Garnish with crumbled blue cheese, if desired. *Makes ¾ cup dip*

Shanghai Red Wings: Combine ¼ cup soy sauce, 3 tablespoons honey, 3 tablespoons Frank's RedHot Sauce, 2 tablespoons peanut oil, 1 teaspoon grated peeled fresh ginger and 1 teaspoon minced garlic in small bowl. Mix well. Pour sauce over wings; toss well to coat evenly.

Cajun Wings: Combine ⅓ cup Frank's RedHot Sauce, ⅓ cup ketchup, ¼ cup (½ stick) melted butter or margarine and 2 teaspoons Cajun seasoning in small bowl. Mix well. Pour sauce over wings; toss well to coat evenly.

Santa Fe Wings: Combine ¼ cup (½ stick) melted butter or margarine, ¼ cup Frank's RedHot Sauce, ¼ cup chili sauce and 1 teaspoon chili powder in small bowl. Mix well. Pour sauce over wings; toss well to coat evenly.

hot artichoke dip

1 package (8 ounces)
PHILADELPHIA®
Cream Cheese, softened
1 can (14 ounces) artichoke
hearts, drained, chopped

½ cup KRAFT® Mayo
Real Mayonnaise
½ cup KRAFT® 100% Grated
Parmesan Cheese
1 clove garlic, minced

MIX all ingredients with electric mixer on medium speed until well blended. Spoon into 9-inch pie plate or quiche dish.

BAKE at 350°F for 20 to 25 minutes or until very lightly browned.

SERVE with NABISCO® Crackers, vegetable dippers or baked pita bread wedges.
Makes 2½ cups

Special Extras: To make baked pita bread wedges, cut each of 3 split pita breads into 8 triangles. Place on cookie sheet. Bake at 350°F for 10 to 12 minutes or until crisp. Makes 48 wedges.

Prep Time: 15 minutes
Bake Time: 25 minutes

hot artichoke dip

tuna in crispy wonton cups

18 wonton skins, each 3¼ inches square

Butter or olive oil cooking spray

1 (2.6-ounce) STARKIST Flavor Fresh Pouch® Tuna (Albacore or Chunk Light)

⅓ cup cold cooked orzo (rice-shaped pasta) or cooked rice

¼ cup southwestern ranch-style vegetable dip with jalapeños or other sour cream dip

¼ cup drained pimiento-stuffed green olives, chopped

3 tablespoons sweet pickle relish, drained

Paprika, for garnish

Parsley sprigs, for garnish

Cut wontons into circles with 3-inch round cookie cutter. Spray miniature muffin pans with cooking spray. Place one circle in each muffin cup; press to sides to mold wonton to cup. Spray each wonton with cooking spray. Bake in 350°F oven 6 to 8 minutes or until golden brown; set aside.

In small bowl, gently mix tuna, orzo, dip, olives and relish. Refrigerate filling until ready to serve. Remove wonton cups from muffin pans. Use rounded teaspoon to fill each cup; garnish with paprika and parsley. *Makes 18 servings*

Tip: These cups can be made one day ahead; store in airtight container. Reheat in 350°F oven 1 to 2 minutes to recrisp.

Prep Time: 20 minutes

caponata

1 pound eggplant, cut into ½-inch cubes

3 large cloves garlic, minced

¼ cup olive oil

1 can (14½ ounces) DEL MONTE® Diced Tomatoes with Basil, Garlic & Oregano

1 medium green pepper, finely chopped

1 can (2¼ ounces) chopped ripe olives, drained

2 tablespoons lemon juice

1 teaspoon dried basil, crushed

1 baguette French bread, cut into ¼-inch slices

1. Cook eggplant and garlic in oil in large skillet over medium heat 5 minutes. Season with salt and pepper, if desired.

2. Stir in remaining ingredients except bread. Cook, uncovered, 10 minutes or until thickened.

3. Cover and chill. Serve with bread. *Makes approximately 4½ cups*

tuna in crispy wonton cups

grilled bruschetta

3 tablespoons olive oil

2 tablespoons red wine vinegar

2 cloves garlic, minced

½ teaspoon cracked black pepper

2 tablespoons chopped fresh parsley or basil leaves

2 medium tomatoes, chopped (about 2 cups)

1 package (11.25 ounces) PEPPERIDGE FARM® Parmesan Texas Toast or Garlic Texas Toast

1. Stir the oil, vinegar, garlic, black pepper, parsley and tomatoes in a medium bowl. Let stand for 15 minutes.

2. Lightly oil the grill rack and heat the grill to medium. Grill the toast slices for 2 minutes or until they're browned on both sides and heated through.

3. Divide the tomato mixture among the toast slices. Serve immediately.

Makes 8 servings

Kitchen Tip: Omit the garlic if using Garlic Texas Toast.

Prep Time: 5 minutes
Stand Time: 15 minutes
Grill Time: 2 minutes

classic fonduta

1 loaf crusty Italian or French bread

¾ cup dry white wine

1 pound BELGIOIOSO® Fontina Cheese, shredded

1 teaspoon cornstarch mixed with 1 teaspoon dry white wine

Black pepper to taste

Cut bread into 1-inch cubes, leaving some crust on each piece. Pour wine into medium saucepan. Heat over medium heat until wine is hot, but not boiling. Add handfuls of BelGioioso Fontina Cheese to wine, stirring constantly with wooden spoon until cheese is melted and mixture has appearance of light, creamy sauce. Stir in cornstarch mixture; boil approximately 30 seconds, adding pepper to taste. Remove saucepan and place on lighted burner on top of table or use fondue pot. Dip bread cubes into cheese mixture using fondue forks.

Makes 4 to 6 servings

grilled bruschetta

easy party meatballs

3 cups (1 pound 10 ounces) PREGO® Marinara Italian Sauce

1 jar (12 ounces) grape jelly

½ cup prepared chili sauce

2½ pounds frozen fully-cooked meatballs, cocktail size

1. Stir the Italian sauce, jelly, chili sauce and meatballs in a 4½-quart slow cooker.

2. Cover and cook on LOW for 6 to 7 hours* or until the meatballs are cooked through. Serve the meatballs on a serving plate with toothpicks. *Makes 8 servings*

Or on HIGH for 3 to 4 hours.

Kitchen Tips: Larger-size or turkey meatballs can also be used, if desired. For a special touch, serve with cranberry chutney for dipping.

Prep Time: 5 minutes
Cook Time: 6 hours
Total Time: 6 hours 5 minutes

crisp tortellini bites

½ cup plain dry bread crumbs

¼ cup grated Parmesan cheese

2 teaspoons HERB-OX® chicken flavored bouillon

¼ teaspoon garlic powder

½ cup sour cream

2 tablespoons milk

1 (9-ounce) package refrigerated cheese-filled tortellini

Warm pizza sauce or marinara sauce, for dipping

Heat oven to 400°F. In small bowl, combine bread crumbs, Parmesan cheese, bouillon and garlic powder. In another small bowl, combine sour cream and milk. Dip tortellini in sour cream mixture, then in bread crumbs; coat evenly. Place tortellini on baking sheet. Bake 10 to 12 minutes or until crisp and golden brown, turning once. Serve immediately with warm pizza or marinara sauce. *Makes 8 servings*

Tip: The bouillon mixture makes a great coating for chicken fingers or mild fish.

easy party meatballs

baked crab rangoon

1 can (6 ounces) white crabmeat, drained, flaked

4 ounces (½ of 8-ounce package) PHILADELPHIA® Neufchâtel Cheese, softened

¼ cup thinly sliced green onions

¼ cup KRAFT® Mayo Light Mayonnaise

12 wonton wrappers

HEAT oven to 350°F. Mix crabmeat, Neufchâtel cheese, onions and mayo.

SPRAY 12 (2½-inch) muffin cups with cooking spray. Gently place 1 wonton wrapper in each cup, allowing edges of wrappers to extend above sides of cups. Fill evenly with crabmeat mixture.

BAKE 18 to 20 minutes or until edges are golden brown and filling is heated through. Serve warm. Garnish with sliced green onions, if desired.

Makes 12 servings (1 wonton each)

Food Facts: Wonton wrappers are usually found in the grocery store in the refrigerated section of the produce department.

Mini Crab Rangoon: Use 24 wonton wrappers. Gently place 1 wonton wrapper in each of 24 miniature muffin cups sprayed with cooking spray. Fill evenly with crabmeat mixture and bake as directed. Makes 12 servings (2 wontons each).

Prep Time: 20 minutes
Bake Time: 20 minutes

crunchy coconut shrimp

1⅓ cups FRENCH'S® French Fried Onions

⅓ cup flaked, sweetened coconut

1 pound large shrimp, shelled and deveined

2 egg whites, beaten

1. Place French Fried Onions and coconut into plastic bag. Lightly crush with hands or rolling pin.

2. Dip shrimp into egg whites. Coat with onion mixture, pressing firmly to adhere.

3. Bake shrimp at 400°F for 10 minutes until shrimp are fully cooked and crispy.

Makes 4 servings

Variation: Add 1 teaspoon curry powder to crushed onions.

Prep Time: 10 minutes
Cook Time: 10 minutes

baked crab rangoon

chipotle-spiced nuts

1 pound mixed nuts
4 tablespoons butter, melted

2 tablespoons ORTEGA®
Chipotle Taco Seasoning Mix
1 tablespoon light brown sugar

Preheat oven to 325°F. Toss nuts, butter, seasoning mix and brown sugar in large bowl until well combined.

Spread nut mixture on baking pan. Bake 20 minutes, stirring after 10 minutes. Serve warm, if desired. To store, allow to cool, and place in airtight container for up to 2 weeks.
Makes 1 pound

Tip: Try sprinkling these nuts over your favorite ice cream for a flavorful "hot" and cold dessert.

Tip: For gift-giving to friends and family, pack these deliciously spicy nuts in a decorative tin can. You can share the recipe on a gift tag, too!

Prep Time: 5 minutes
Start to Finish Time: 25 minutes

the famous lipton® california dip

1 envelope LIPTON®
RECIPE SECRETS®
Onion Soup Mix

1 container (16 ounces)
sour cream

Blend soup mix with sour cream in small bowl; chill at least 2 hours. Serve with your favorite dippers.
Makes about 2 cups dip

Tip: For a creamier dip, add more sour cream.

Sensational Spinach Dip: Add 1 package (10 ounces) frozen chopped spinach, thawed and squeezed dry.

California Seafood Dip: Add 1 cup finely chopped cooked clams, crabmeat or shrimp, ¼ cup chili sauce and 1 tablespoon horseradish.

California Bacon Dip: Add ⅓ cup crumbled cooked bacon or bacon bits.

California Blue Cheese Dip: Add ¼ pound crumbled blue cheese and ¼ cup finely chopped walnuts.

chipotle-spiced nuts

thai pizza

1 package **JENNIE-O TURKEY STORE®** Breast Strips

2 teaspoons bottled or fresh minced ginger

2 teaspoons bottled or fresh minced garlic

¼ teaspoon crushed red pepper flakes

Cooking spray

¼ cup hoisin or stir-fry sauce

1 large (12-inch) prepared pizza crust

⅓ cup thinly sliced green onions

½ teaspoon finely grated lime peel

⅓ cup coarsely chopped roasted peanuts

2 tablespoons chopped cilantro or basil

Heat oven to 450°F. Toss turkey strips with ginger, garlic and pepper flakes. Coat large nonstick skillet with cooking spray; heat over medium-high heat. Add turkey; stir-fry 2 minutes. Add hoisin sauce; stir-fry 2 minutes. Place pizza crust on large cookie sheet. Spread mixture evenly over pizza crust; sprinkle with green onions and lime peel. Bake 8 to 10 minutes or until crust is golden brown and hot. Sprinkle with peanuts and cilantro. Cut into wedges. *Makes 12 appetizer or 6 main-dish servings*

Prep Time: 15 minutes
Cook Time: 15 minutes

marinated mushrooms

2 pounds mushrooms

1 bottle (8 ounces) Italian salad dressing

Grated peel of ½ **SUNKIST®** lemon

Juice of 1 **SUNKIST®** lemon

2 tablespoons sliced pimiento (optional)

2 tablespoons chopped fresh parsley

In large saucepan, combine mushrooms and Italian dressing; bring to a boil. Cook, uncovered, 2 to 3 minutes, stirring constantly. Add lemon peel, juice and pimiento. Chill 4 hours or more. Drain, reserving dressing for another use. Stir parsley into mushrooms. Serve as an appetizer with toothpicks. Garnish with lemon cartwheel slices, if desired. *Makes about 4 cups*

Note: Reserved dressing may be used on salads. Makes about 1½ cups.

Variation: Substitute 1 bottle (8 ounces) reduced-calorie Italian dressing for regular Italian dressing.

fried calamari

Vegetable oil for frying
¾ cup **CREAM OF WHEAT**®
Hot Cereal (Instant,
1-minute, 2½-minute or
10-minute cook time),
uncooked
¾ cup grated Parmesan cheese
1 teaspoon salt

1 pound frozen calamari,
thawed, cleaned
½ cup cornstarch
1 cup cold water
Fresh lemon wedges (optional)
Marinara sauce (optional)

1. Preheat oil in deep fryer or heavy saucepan to 360°F. Combine Cream of Wheat, cheese and salt in shallow bowl; set aside.

2. Cut tubes of calamari into ½-inch rings; remove long tentacles. Pat dry with paper towel. Toss rings and tentacles in cornstarch to evenly coat. Dip briefly into cold water, then toss in Cream of Wheat mixture to evenly coat.

3. Place in hot oil. Cook 3 to 4 minutes or until the rings begin to brown. Remove with slotted spoon and drain on paper towels. Serve warm with lemon wedges and warm marinara sauce for dipping, if desired. *Makes 4 servings*

Tip: These crunchy rings are addictive, but you can double this recipe so everyone has plenty to munch.

Prep Time: 5 minutes
Start to Finish Time: 10 minutes

guacamole

2 avocados, mashed
¼ cup red salsa (mild or hot,
according to taste)
3 tablespoons **NEWMAN'S
OWN**® Salad Dressing

2 tablespoons lime or lemon
juice
1 clove garlic, finely minced
Salt and black pepper

Combine all ingredients and mix well. Chill for 1 to 2 hours tightly covered. Serve with tortilla chips. *Makes about 2 cups*

fried calamari

slow-cooked pulled pork sliders

1 can (10¾ ounces)
  CAMPBELL'S®
  Condensed Tomato Soup
½ cup packed brown sugar
¼ cup cider vinegar
1 teaspoon garlic powder

1 boneless pork shoulder roast
  (3½ to 4½ pounds)
2 packages (15 ounces each)
  PEPPERIDGE FARM®
  Slider Mini Sandwich Rolls
Hot pepper sauce (optional)

1. Stir the soup, brown sugar, vinegar and garlic powder in a 6-quart slow cooker. Add the pork and turn to coat.

2. Cover and cook on LOW for 8 to 9 hours* or until the pork is fork-tender. Spoon off any fat.

3. Remove the pork from the cooker to a cutting board and let stand for 10 minutes. Using 2 forks, shred the pork. Return the pork to the cooker.

4. Divide the pork mixture among the rolls. Serve with the hot pepper sauce, if desired.

Makes 12 mini sandwiches

Or on HIGH for 5 to 6 hours.

Prep Time: 10 minutes
Cook Time: 8 hours
Stand Time: 10 minutes

deviled eggs

1 dozen eggs
½ cup plain lowfat
  STONYFIELD FARM®
  Yogurt
1 tablespoon Dijon mustard

1 teaspoon lemon juice
1 teaspoon paprika
Fresh chopped chives
  for garnish

Place eggs in large saucepan and cover with cold water. Bring water to a boil and immediately remove from heat. Cover and let eggs stand in hot water for 10 to 12 minutes. Remove from hot water, cool and peel. Slice eggs in half lengthwise and remove yolks. Place yolks in medium bowl. Mash together with yogurt, mustard and lemon juice. Fill hollowed egg whites generously with egg yolk mixture. Sprinkle with paprika and chives. Refrigerate until ready to serve.   *Makes 24 servings*

slow-cooked pulled pork sliders

zesty crab cakes with red pepper sauce

½ pound raw medium shrimp, shelled and deveined

⅔ cup heavy cream

1 egg white

3 tablespoons FRANK'S® REDHOT® Original Cayenne Pepper Sauce

1 tablespoon FRENCH'S® Worcestershire Sauce

¼ teaspoon seasoned salt

1 pound crabmeat or imitation crabmeat, flaked (4 cups)

1 red or yellow bell pepper, minced

2 green onions, minced

¼ cup minced fresh parsley

1½ cups fresh bread crumbs

½ cup corn oil

Red Pepper Sauce (recipe follows)

1. Place shrimp, cream, egg white, Frank's RedHot Sauce, Worcestershire and seasoned salt in food processor. Process until mixture is puréed. Transfer to large bowl.

2. Add crabmeat, bell pepper, onions and parsley. Mix with fork until well blended.

3. Shape crabmeat mixture into 12 (½-inch-thick) patties, using about ¼ cup mixture for each. Coat both sides in bread crumbs.

4. Heat oil in large nonstick skillet. Add crab cakes; cook until browned on both sides. Drain on paper towels. Serve with Red Pepper Sauce.

Makes about 1 dozen crab cakes

Prep Time: 30 minutes
Cook Time: 15 minutes

red pepper sauce

1 jar (7 ounces) roasted red peppers, drained

¼ cup mayonnaise

3 tablespoons FRANK'S® REDHOT® Original Cayenne Pepper Sauce

2 tablespoons minced onion

1 tablespoon FRENCH'S® Spicy Brown Mustard

1 tablespoon minced parsley

1 clove garlic

Place all ingredients in blender or food processor. Cover; blend until smooth.

Makes 1 cup sauce

zesty crab cakes with red pepper sauce

bbq orange wings

8 TYSON® Individually Frozen
Chicken Wings

½ cup bottled barbecue sauce

½ cup orange marmalade, or
plum or pineapple preserves

Salt and black pepper, to taste

1. Preheat oven to 400°F. Line 13×9-inch baking pan with foil; spray with nonstick cooking spray. Wash hands. Arrange frozen wings in single layer in pan. Wash hands. Combine barbecue sauce and marmalade; reserve half of mixture to serve with cooked wings.

2. Bake wings 20 minutes; drain and discard juices. Sprinkle wings with salt and pepper. Bake an additional 20 minutes. Turn over wings and baste with sauce. Bake 15 to 20 minutes more or until internal juices of chicken run clear. (Or insert instant-read meat thermometer into thickest part of chicken. Temperature should read 180°F.)

3. Heat reserved sauce and serve with wings. Refrigerate leftovers immediately.

Makes 4 servings

Prep Time: 5 minutes
Cook Time: 1 hour

hearty game day potato skins

6 large baking potatoes (about
3¾ pounds), unpeeled and
baked

3 tablespoons PROMISE®
Buttery Spread, melted

¾ cup low-fat Cheddar cheese
(about 3 ounces)

2 large tomatoes, chopped

½ cup light sour cream

2 large green onions, finely
chopped

1. Preheat oven to 425°F.

2. Cut cooked potatoes in half lengthwise. Remove about ⅓ of potato pulp, leaving ½-inch shell (save pulp for another use), then cut potatoes in half crosswise. Brush inside of each potato and skin with PROMISE® Buttery Spread.

3. On baking sheet, arrange potatoes. Bake 15 minutes or until potatoes are crisp. Evenly top with cheese and tomatoes. Broil 1 minute or until cheese is melted. Top with sour cream, then sprinkle with green onions. *Makes 24 servings*

Prep Time: 1 hour
Cook Time: 17 minutes

cocktail wraps

16 **HILLSHIRE FARM®** Lit'l
Smokies® Cocktail Links
16 thin strips Cheddar, Swiss or
hot pepper cheese

1 package (8 ounces) refrigerated
crescent roll dough
Mustard (optional)

1. Preheat oven to 400°F. Cut a thin slit in each sausage. Place 1 cheese strip inside slit of each sausage.

2. Separate crescent roll dough into 8 triangles. Cut each triangle in half lengthwise to form 2 smaller triangles. Place 1 sausage on wide end of triangle and roll towards the point. Place wrapped sausage, point side down, on baking sheet. Repeat with remaining sausages.

3. Bake 9 to 10 minutes or until golden brown. Serve with mustard, if desired.

Makes 8 appetizer servings (2 Lit'l Smokies® each)

baked brie with apricot chutney

½ cup chopped pear
¼ cup **POLANER®** Sugar Free
Apricot or Sugar Free
Pineapple Preserves
2 tablespoons finely chopped
red bell pepper
2 tablespoons chopped onion

2 tablespoons raisins
1 tablespoon vinegar
¼ teaspoon each ground ginger
and cinnamon
1 (13- to 16-ounce) round Brie
cheese
2 tablespoons chopped cashews

Combine all ingredients except cheese and cashews in small pan over medium heat; bring to a boil, stirring frequently. Reduce heat to low; simmer 15 to 20 minutes until thickened, stirring occasionally. Cool or refrigerate up to 3 days.

Heat oven to 350°F.

Place Brie in shallow ovenproof dish; top with chutney.

Bake 15 to 20 minutes until cheese softens and is heated through.

Sprinkle with cashews. Serve with whole grain crackers or apple slices.

Makes 10 servings

Prep Time: 15 minutes
Cook Time: 20 minutes
Bake Time: 15 minutes

cocktail wraps

cool veggie pizza appetizer

2 cans (8 ounces each)
refrigerated crescent
dinner rolls

1 package (8 ounces)
PHILADELPHIA®
Cream Cheese, softened

½ cup MIRACLE WHIP®
Dressing

1 teaspoon dill weed

½ teaspoon onion salt

1 cup broccoli florets

1 cup chopped green bell pepper

1 cup chopped seeded tomato

¼ cup chopped red onion

HEAT oven to 375°F. Separate dough into 4 rectangles. Press onto bottom and up side of 15×10×1-inch baking pan to form crust.

BAKE 11 to 13 minutes or until golden brown; cool.

MIX cream cheese, dressing, dill and onion salt until well blended. Spread over crust; top with remaining ingredients. Refrigerate. Cut into squares.   *Makes 32 servings*

Prep Time: 20 minutes plus refrigerating
Bake Time: 13 minutes

open-faced reubens

1 box (6 ounces) rye Melba toast
rounds

¼ pound thinly sliced cooked
corned beef, cut into ½-inch
squares

1 can (8 ounces) sauerkraut,
rinsed, drained and chopped

1 cup (4 ounces) finely shredded
Wisconsin Swiss cheese

2 teaspoons prepared mustard
Caraway seeds

Preheat oven to 350°F. Arrange toast rounds on baking sheets. Top each with 1 beef square and 1 teaspoon sauerkraut. Combine cheese and mustard in small bowl; spoon about 1 teaspoon cheese mixture on top of sauerkraut. Sprinkle with caraway seeds. Bake about 5 minutes or until cheese is melted.   *Makes about 48 appetizer servings*

Microwave Directions: Arrange 8 toast rounds around edge of microwave-safe plate lined with paper towel. Place 2 rounds in center. Top as directed. Microwave, uncovered, on MEDIUM (50% power) 1 to 2 minutes until cheese is melted, turning plate once. Repeat with remaining ingredients.

Favorite recipe from **Wisconsin Milk Marketing Board**

cool veggie pizza appetizer

ginger plum spareribs

1 jar (10 ounces) damson plum
    preserves or apple jelly
⅓ cup KARO® Light or Dark
    Corn Syrup
⅓ cup soy sauce
¼ cup chopped green onions

2 cloves garlic, minced
2 teaspoons ground ginger
2 pounds pork spareribs,
    trimmed, cut into serving
    pieces

1. In small saucepan, combine preserves, corn syrup, soy sauce, green onions, garlic and ginger. Stirring constantly, cook over medium heat until melted and smooth.

2. Pour into 11×7×2-inch baking dish. Add ribs, turning to coat. Cover; refrigerate several hours or overnight, turning once.

3. Remove ribs from marinade; place on rack in shallow baking pan.

4. Bake in 350°F oven about 1 hour or until tender, turning occasionally and basting with marinade. Do not baste during last 5 minutes of cooking.

Makes about 20 appetizer or 4 main-dish servings

Ginger Plum Chicken Wings: Omit spareribs. Follow recipe for Ginger Plum Spareribs. Use 2½ pounds chicken wings, separated at the joints (tips discarded). Bake 45 minutes, basting with marinade during last 30 minutes.

Prep Time: 15 minutes plus marinating
Bake Time: 1 hour

spicy cream cheese roll-ups

8 ounces (1 package) fat-free
    or low-fat cream cheese,
    softened
3 tablespoons chopped green
    onions

2 tablespoons finely chopped
    red pepper
2 tablespoons MRS. DASH®
    Southwest Chipotle
    Seasoning Blend
4 large flour tortillas

1. In a medium bowl, combine all ingredients except tortillas.

2. Spread a thin layer of cream cheese mixture on each flour tortilla. Starting at one end, gently roll tortillas into a tight tube. Wrap and chill until ready to serve.

3. To serve, unwrap roll, trim edges of tortilla and cut into eight 1-inch slices. Serve slices on their side on a colorful platter.

Makes 16 servings

Prep Time: 10 minutes

ginger plum spareribs

soups & stews

ravioli soup

1 package (9 ounces) fresh or
frozen cheese ravioli or
tortellini

¾ pound hot Italian sausage,
crumbled

1 can (14½ ounces)
DEL MONTE® Italian
Recipe Stewed Tomatoes

1 can (14½ ounces) beef broth

1 can (14½ ounces)
DEL MONTE® Cut Italian
Green Beans, drained

2 green onions, sliced

1. Cook pasta according to package directions; drain.

2. Meanwhile, cook sausage in 5-quart pot over medium-high heat until no longer pink; drain. Add undrained tomatoes, broth and 1¾ cups water; bring to a boil.

3. Reduce heat to low; stir in pasta, beans and green onions. Simmer until heated through. Season with pepper and sprinkle with grated Parmesan cheese, if desired.

Makes 4 servings

Prep and Cook Time: 15 minutes

hearty meatball stew

1 pound ground turkey breast or
extra-lean ground beef

¾ cup QUAKER® Oats (quick
or old fashioned, uncooked)

1 can (8 ounces) no-salt-added
tomato sauce, divided

1½ teaspoons garlic powder

1½ teaspoons dried thyme leaves,
divided

2 cans (14½ ounces each)
reduced-sodium, fat-free
chicken broth

¾ teaspoon salt (optional)

2½ cups any frozen vegetable
blend (do not thaw)

⅓ cup ditalini or other small
pasta

¼ cup water

2 tablespoons cornstarch

1. Heat broiler. Lightly spray rack of broiler pan with nonstick cooking spray.

2. Combine turkey, oats, ⅓ cup tomato sauce, garlic powder and 1 teaspoon thyme in large bowl; mix lightly but thoroughly. Transfer to sheet of aluminum foil or waxed paper. Pat mixture into 9×6-inch rectangle. Cut into 1½-inch squares; roll each square into a ball. Arrange meatballs on broiler pan.

3. Broil meatballs 6 to 8 inches from heat about 6 minutes or until cooked through, turning once.

4. While meatballs cook, bring broth, remaining tomato sauce, remaining ½ teaspoon thyme and salt, if desired, to a boil in 4-quart saucepan or Dutch oven over medium-high heat. Add vegetables and pasta; return to a boil. Reduce heat, cover and simmer 10 minutes or until vegetables and pasta are tender. Stir together water and cornstarch in small bowl until smooth. Add to pan along with meatballs. Cook and stir until broth is thickened. Spoon into bowls. *Makes 6 servings*

sausage & zucchini soup

1 pound BOB EVANS®
Italian Roll Sausage

1 medium onion, diced

1 (28-ounce) can stewed tomatoes

2 (14-ounce) cans beef broth

2 medium zucchini, diced or
sliced (about 2 cups)

2 small carrots, diced

2 stalks celery, diced

4 large mushrooms, sliced

Grated Parmesan cheese
for garnish

Crumble and cook sausage and onion in large saucepan over medium heat until sausage is browned. Drain off any drippings. Add remaining ingredients except cheese; simmer, uncovered, over low heat about 40 minutes or until vegetables are tender. Garnish with cheese. Refrigerate leftovers. *Makes 8 servings*

hearty meatball stew

country noodle soup

1 tablespoon I CAN'T
BELIEVE IT'S NOT
BUTTER!® Spread
¾ cup finely chopped onion
½ cup finely chopped red bell
pepper
4 cups chicken broth or bouillon

2½ cups water
1 package KNORR® PASTA
SIDES™–Chicken Broccoli
or Chicken
½ cup cut-up cooked chicken,
turkey or ham (optional)

Melt I Can't Believe It's Not Butter!® Spread in 4-quart saucepan over medium-high heat and cook onion and red pepper, stirring occasionally, 5 minutes or until tender. Stir in chicken broth and water. Bring just to a boil over high heat. Stir in Knorr® Pasta Sides™–Chicken Broccoli. Continue boiling over medium heat, stirring occasionally, 8 minutes or until pasta is tender. Stir in chicken; heat through.   *Makes 6 servings*

Tip: Also delicious as a warm after-school pick-me-up!

Prep Time: 10 minutes
Cook Time: 16 minutes

burgundy beef stew

¾ pound beef sirloin steak,
cut into 1-inch cubes
1 cup diagonally sliced carrots
1 teaspoon minced garlic
¼ cup Burgundy or other dry
red wine
2⅓ cups canned beef broth

1 can (14½ ounces)
DEL MONTE® Diced
Tomatoes, undrained
1 box rice pilaf mix
1 jar (15 ounces) whole pearl
onions, drained

1. Generously spray large saucepan or Dutch oven with nonstick cooking spray. Heat over high heat until hot. Add beef; cook 2 to 3 minutes or until no longer pink. Stir in carrots, garlic and wine; cook 2 minutes.

2. Add broth, tomatoes, rice and contents of seasoning packet. Bring to a boil. Cover; reduce heat and simmer 10 minutes, stirring occasionally. Add onions; cook 10 minutes more or until rice is tender. Remove from heat and let stand, covered, 5 minutes.
     Makes 4 servings

Variation: One 15-ounce can of drained sweet peas and pearl onions can be substituted for the pearl onions.

country noodle soup

cincinnati chili

1½ pounds ground beef

2 large onions, chopped
(about 2 cups)

¼ teaspoon garlic powder or
2 cloves garlic, minced

2 teaspoons chili powder

¼ teaspoon ground cinnamon

Dash ground cloves

4 cups CAMPBELL'S®
Tomato Juice

2 cans (about 15 ounces each)
kidney beans, drained

Hot cooked spaghetti

1. Cook beef, onions and garlic powder in saucepot over medium-high heat in 2 batches until beef is browned and onion is tender, stirring to separate the meat. Remove beef and onion. Pour off fat. Return beef and onion to saucepot.

2. Stir in chili powder, cinnamon and cloves and cook 2 minutes. Stir in tomato juice. Heat to a boil. Cover and cook over low heat 30 minutes.

3. Add beans. Cover and cook 15 minutes, stirring occasionally. Serve over spaghetti.

Makes 8 servings

Prep Time: 10 minutes
Cook Time: 1 hour
Total Time: 1 hour 10 minutes

harvest soup

½ pound BOB EVANS® Special
Seasonings Roll Sausage

1 large onion, finely chopped

2½ cups chicken broth

2 cups canned pumpkin

2 cups hot milk

1 teaspoon lemon juice

Dash ground nutmeg

Dash ground cinnamon

Salt and black pepper to taste

Chopped fresh parsley

Crumble and cook sausage and onion in large saucepan until sausage is browned. Drain off any drippings. Add broth and bring to a boil. Stir in pumpkin; cover and simmer over low heat 15 to 20 minutes. Add milk, lemon juice, nutmeg, cinnamon, salt and pepper; simmer, uncovered, 5 minutes to blend flavors. Sprinkle with parsley before serving. Refrigerate leftovers.

Makes 6 to 8 servings

cincinnati chili

chicken & herb dumplings

2 pounds skinless, boneless
   chicken breasts and/or
   thighs, cut into 1-inch pieces

5 medium carrots, cut into 1-inch
   pieces (about 2½ cups)

4 stalks celery, cut into 1-inch
   pieces (about 2 cups)

2 cups frozen whole kernel corn

3½ cups SWANSON®
   Chicken Stock

¼ teaspoon ground black pepper

¼ cup all-purpose flour

½ cup water

2 cups all-purpose baking mix

⅔ cup milk

1 tablespoon chopped fresh
   rosemary leaves or
   1 teaspoon dried rosemary
   leaves, crushed

1. Stir the chicken, carrots, celery, corn, stock and black pepper in a 6-quart slow cooker.

2. Cover and cook on LOW for 7 to 8 hours* or until the chicken is cooked through.

3. Stir the flour and water in a small bowl until the mixture is smooth. Stir the flour mixture in the cooker. Turn the heat to HIGH. Cover and cook for 5 minutes or until the mixture boils and thickens.

4. Stir the baking mix, milk and rosemary in a medium bowl. Drop the batter by rounded tablespoonfuls over the chicken mixture. Tilt the lid to vent and cook on HIGH for 40 minutes or until the dumplings are cooked in the center.

Makes 8 servings

Or on HIGH for 4 to 5 hours.

Prep Time: 20 minutes
Cook Time: 7 hours 45 minutes
Total Time: 8 hours 5 minutes

tip: *Leaving the lid of the slow cooker slightly ajar prevents condensation from dripping onto the dumplings during cooking.*

chicken & herb dumplings

italian veg•all® stew

2 tablespoons butter
1 cup diced onion
1 cup shredded cabbage
2 cups water
2 cans (14½ ounces each) stewed tomatoes
1 can (15 ounces) VEG•ALL® Original Mixed Vegetables, drained

1 tablespoon chopped fresh parsley
½ teaspoon dried basil
½ teaspoon dried oregano
½ teaspoon black pepper

In large saucepan, melt butter. Stir in onion and cabbage. Heat for 2 minutes. Add water; cover and simmer for 10 minutes. Stir in tomatoes, Veg•All and seasonings. Simmer for 10 minutes.

Makes 6 servings

homestyle ham & bean soup

1 large yellow onion, chopped
1 cup sliced carrots
1 cup sliced celery
2 cloves minced garlic
2 tablespoons olive or vegetable oil
6 cups chicken broth

2 (15-ounce) cans great Northern beans
2 (5-ounce) cans HORMEL® chunk ham
¼ teaspoon ground white pepper
¼ teaspoon dried thyme leaves
Chopped fresh parsley (optional)

In 5-quart saucepan, sauté onion, carrots, celery and garlic in oil until golden, about 5 to 7 minutes. Add chicken broth, beans, ham, white pepper and thyme. Heat and stir until warmed through, about 15 minutes. Ladle soup into bowls and serve. If desired, top with chopped fresh parsley.

Makes 8 servings

Serving Suggestion: To add extra kick to your ham and bean soup, serve it with hot pepper sauce on the side.

Variation: If you have a leftover baked potato, simply dice and add to your ham and bean soup.

italian veg•all® stew

manhattan clam chowder

¼ cup chopped bacon
1 cup chopped onion
½ cup chopped carrots
½ cup chopped celery
2 cans (14.5 ounces each) CONTADINA® Diced Tomatoes, undrained
1 can (8 ounces) CONTADINA® Tomato Sauce

1 bottle (8 ounces) clam juice
1 large bay leaf
½ teaspoon chopped fresh rosemary
⅛ teaspoon black pepper
2 cans (6.5 ounces each) chopped clams, undrained

1. Sauté bacon with onion, carrots and celery in large saucepan.

2. Stir in undrained tomatoes with remaining ingredients, except clams. Heat to boiling. Reduce heat; boil gently 15 minutes. Stir in clams and juice.

3. Heat additional 5 minutes. Remove bay leaf before serving. *Makes 6½ cups*

Microwave Directions: Combine bacon, onion, carrots and celery in 2-quart microwave-safe casserole dish. Microwave on HIGH (100%) power 5 minutes. Stir in remaining ingredients, except clams. Microwave on HIGH power 5 minutes. Stir in clams and juice. Microwave on HIGH power 5 minutes. Remove bay leaf before serving.

quick & easy chili

1 package JENNIE-O TURKEY STORE® Lean Ground Turkey
1 tablespoon chili powder
1 tablespoon dried onion
2 teaspoons bottled minced garlic

2 cans (15½ ounces each) chili beans in spicy sauce, undrained
1 can (14½ ounces) salsa-style or chili-style tomatoes, undrained
Optional toppings: shredded Cheddar cheese, sour cream, chopped cilantro

Crumble turkey into large saucepan; add chili powder, onion and garlic. Cook over medium-high heat 5 minutes, stirring occasionally. Add beans and tomatoes; bring to a simmer. Simmer uncovered 10 minutes, stirring occasionally. Serve with desired toppings. *Makes 6 servings*

manhattan clam chowder

slow cooker beef & mushroom stew

1 boneless beef bottom round
   roast or chuck pot roast
   (about 1½ pounds), cut
   into 1-inch pieces

Ground black pepper

¼ cup all-purpose flour

2 tablespoons vegetable oil

1 can (10½ ounces)
   CAMPBELL'S® Condensed
   French Onion Soup

1 cup Burgundy or other dry
   red wine

2 cloves garlic, minced

1 teaspoon Italian seasoning,
   crushed

10 ounces mushrooms, cut in half
   (about 3 cups)

3 medium carrots, cut into 2-inch
   pieces (about 1½ cups)

1 cup frozen whole small white
   onions

¼ cup water

1. Season the beef with the black pepper. Coat the beef with **2 tablespoons** flour. Heat the oil in a 12-inch skillet over medium-high heat. Add the beef and cook until it's well browned, stirring often.

2. Stir the beef, soup, wine, garlic, Italian seasoning, mushrooms, carrots and onions in a 3½-quart slow cooker.

3. Cover and cook on LOW for 10 to 11 hours* or until the beef is fork-tender.

4. Stir the remaining flour and water in a small bowl until the mixture is smooth. Stir the flour mixture in the cooker. Increase the heat to HIGH. Cover and cook for 15 minutes or until the mixture boils and thickens.   *Makes 6 servings*

*Or on HIGH for 5 to 6 hours.

Serving Suggestion: Serve with a mixed green salad tossed with shredded carrots, chopped tomatoes, cucumbers and balsamic vinaigrette and crusty Italian bread. For dessert serve cranberry-apple crisp topped with vanilla ice cream.

Prep Time: 20 minutes
Cook Time: 10 hours 15 minutes
Total Time: 10 hours 35 minutes

slow cooker beef & mushroom stew

roasted sweet potato soup

5 medium sweet potatoes
(about 2 pounds)

2 tablespoons butter

1 medium onion, chopped
(about 1 cup)

2 stalks celery, chopped
(about 1 cup)

6 cups SWANSON® Chicken
Broth (Regular, Natural
Goodness® or Certified
Organic)

1 medium potato, peeled and cut
into cubes (about 1 cup)

⅓ cup maple syrup

⅛ teaspoon ground white pepper

2 tablespoons light cream
(optional)

1. Pierce the sweet potatoes with a fork. Microwave on HIGH for 8 to 13 minutes or bake at 400°F. for 1 hour or until they're fork-tender. Cut in half lengthwise. Scoop out sweet potato pulp and set aside.

2. Heat the butter in a 6-quart saucepot over medium heat. Add the onion and celery to the saucepot and cook until tender. Add the broth and potato. Heat to a boil. Reduce the heat to low. Cook for 15 minutes or until the potato is tender. Add the maple syrup, white pepper and reserved sweet potato.

3. Place ⅓ of the broth mixture into an electric blender or food processor container. Cover and blend until smooth. Pour the mixture into a large bowl. Repeat the blending process twice more with the remaining broth mixture. Return all of the puréed mixture to the saucepot. Add the cream, if desired. Cook over medium heat until the mixture is hot. Season to taste.   *Makes 8 servings*

Prep Time: 30 minutes
Cook Time: 20 minutes

tip: *To save time, substitute 3¾ cups mashed drained canned sweet potatoes for the fresh sweet potatoes.*

roasted sweet potato soup

super chili for a crowd

2 large onions, chopped

1 tablespoon minced garlic

2 pounds boneless top round or sirloin steak, cut into ½-inch cubes

1 pound ground beef

1 can (28 ounces) crushed tomatoes in purée

1 can (15 to 19 ounces) red kidney beans, undrained

⅓ cup FRANK'S® REDHOT® Original Cayenne Pepper Sauce

2 packages (1¼ ounces each) chili seasoning mix

1. Heat *1 tablespoon oil* in 5-quart saucepot or Dutch oven until hot. Sauté onions and garlic until tender; transfer to bowl.

2. Heat *3 tablespoons oil* in same pot; cook meat in batches until well browned. Drain fat.

3. Add *¾ cup water* and remaining ingredients to pot. Stir in onion and garlic. Heat to boiling, stirring. Simmer, partially covered, for 1 hour or until meat is tender, stirring often. Garnish as desired. *Makes 10 servings*

Prep Time: 15 minutes
Cook Time: 1 hour 15 minutes

classic onion soup

4 large yellow onions (about 9 to 11 ounces each), sliced

6 tablespoons butter or margarine

1 tablespoon sugar

2 quarts (8 cups) reduced-sodium chicken broth

½ cup brandy (optional)

Salt and black pepper to taste

½ baguette French bread, cut into slices and toasted

Grated Romano cheese

Melt butter in 4-quart saucepan or Dutch oven. Add onions; cook over medium heat 12 minutes, stirring often, or until tender and golden. Add sugar and cook, stirring for 1 minute. Add broth; cover and bring to a boil. Reduce heat; simmer 12 minutes. If desired, add brandy; cook 2 minutes longer. Season with salt and pepper. To serve, ladle soup into bowl; float toast on top. Sprinkle with cheese. *Makes 6 servings*

Favorite recipe from **National Onion Association**

super chili for a crowd

black bean and bacon soup

5 strips bacon, sliced

1 medium onion, diced

2 tablespoons ORTEGA® Fire-
Roasted Diced Green Chiles

2 cans (15 ounces each)
ORTEGA® Black Beans,
undrained

4 cups chicken broth

½ cup ORTEGA® Taco Sauce

½ cup sour cream

4 ORTEGA® Yellow Corn
Taco Shells, crumbled

Cook bacon in large pot over medium heat 5 minutes or until crisp. Add onion and chiles. Cook 5 minutes or until onion begins to brown. Stir in beans, broth and taco sauce. Bring to a boil. Reduce heat to low. Simmer 20 minutes.

Purée half of soup in food processor until smooth (or use immersion blender in pot). Return puréed soup to pot and stir to combine. Serve with a dollop of sour cream and crumbled taco shells. *Makes 6 to 8 servings*

Note: For a less chunky soup, purée the entire batch and cook an additional 15 minutes.

chunky beef chili

1½ pounds beef for stew, cut into
1- to 1½-inch pieces

2 tablespoons oil, divided

Salt

1 medium onion, chopped

1 jalapeño pepper, minced

2 cans (about 14 ounces each)
chili-seasoned diced
tomatoes

1. Heat 1 tablespoon oil in stockpot over medium heat until hot. Brown ½ of beef; remove from stockpot. Repeat with remaining beef. Remove beef from stockpot. Season with salt, as desired.

2. Add remaining 1 tablespoon oil, onion and jalapeño pepper to stockpot. Cook and stir 5 to 8 minutes or until vegetables are tender. Return beef and juices to stockpot. Add tomatoes; bring to a boil. Reduce heat; cover tightly and simmer 1¾ to 2¼ hours or until beef is fork-tender. *Makes 4 servings*

Cook's Tip: Canned Mexican or Southwest-style diced tomatoes may be substituted for chili-seasoned tomatoes.

Prep and Cook Time: 2 to 2¾ hours

Favorite recipe from **Courtesy The Beef Checkoff**

black bean and bacon soup

hearty one-pot chicken stew

12 TYSON® Individually Frozen Boneless Skinless Chicken Tenderloins

1 box traditional red beans and rice mix

2¼ cups water

1 can (14½ ounces) diced tomatoes, undrained

3 new red potatoes, unpeeled, cut into 1-inch pieces

2 carrots, sliced ½ inch thick

1 onion, cut into 1-inch pieces

1. Wash hands. Remove protective ice glaze from frozen chicken by holding under cool running water 1 to 2 minutes. Cut into 1-inch pieces. Wash hands.

2. In large saucepan, combine chicken, beans and rice, contents of seasoning packet, water, tomatoes, potatoes, carrots and onion. Bring to a boil. Cover and reduce heat; simmer 20 minutes or until internal juices of chicken run clear. (Or insert instant-read meat thermometer into thickest part of chicken. Temperature should read 180°F.) Refrigerate leftovers immediately. *Makes 4 servings*

Serving Suggestion: Serve with hot rolls and a salad of mixed greens.

Prep Time: 10 minutes
Cook Time: 20 to 25 minutes

cajun shrimp and potato chowder

1 tablespoon olive oil

½ pound medium shrimp (26 to 30 count), peeled, deveined (thawed if frozen)

½ cup chopped onion

½ cup chopped green bell pepper

2 cups SIMPLY POTATOES® Homestyle Slices, chopped slightly

1 can (14 ounces) chicken broth

2 teaspoons Cajun seasoning

2 tablespoons all-purpose flour

2 tablespoons water

1 can (14½ ounces) diced tomatoes, undrained

1. Heat oil in 2-quart saucepan over medium heat. Add shrimp, onion and green pepper. Cook, stirring occasionally, until shrimp are no longer pink. Add Simply Potatoes®, broth and Cajun seasoning. Bring to a boil. Reduce heat to low. Cook, stirring occasionally, until Simply Potatoes® are tender (20 to 25 minutes).

2. In small bowl, combine flour and water; stir until smooth. Add flour mixture to soup. Stir in tomatoes. Cook until mixture is thickened and heated through. *Makes 4 servings*

Total Time: 35 minutes

hearty one-pot chicken stew

chick-pea and shrimp soup

1 tablespoon olive or
vegetable oil

1 cup diced onion

2 cloves garlic, minced

4 cans (10.5 ounces each) beef
broth

1 can (14.5 ounces)
CONTADINA® Diced
Tomatoes with Roasted
Garlic, undrained

1 can (15 ounces) chick-peas or
garbanzo beans, drained

1 can (6 ounces) CONTADINA®
Italian Paste with Italian
Herbs

8 ounces small cooked shrimp

2 tablespoons chopped fresh
Italian parsley or 2 teaspoons
dried parsley flakes, crushed

½ teaspoon salt

¼ teaspoon ground black pepper

1. Heat oil over medium-high heat in large saucepan. Add onion and garlic; sauté
for 1 minute.

2. Stir in broth, undrained tomatoes, chick-peas and tomato paste. Bring to boil.

3. Reduce heat to low; simmer, uncovered, 10 minutes. Add shrimp, parsley, salt
and pepper; simmer 3 minutes or until heated through. Stir before serving.

Makes 8 to 10 servings

easy sausage soup

1 package HILLSHIRE FARM®
Smoked Sausage

4 cups chicken broth

1 jar (16 ounces) mild or
medium salsa

1 cup sliced fresh mushrooms

1 package (9 ounces) refrigerated
cheese tortellini

1. Cut sausage in ¼-inch slices. In a large saucepan combine sausage, broth, salsa and
mushrooms. Bring to a boil, reduce heat and simmer 10 minutes.

2. Add tortellini, return to a boil and simmer 15 minutes.

Makes 8 servings (about 1 cup each)

chick-pea and shrimp soup

slow-cooked panama pork stew

2 cups SWANSON® Chicken Broth (Regular, Natural Goodness® or Certified Organic)

4 medium sweet potatoes, peeled and cut into 2-inch pieces

2 medium green peppers, cut into 1-inch pieces (about 2 cups)

1½ cups frozen whole kernel corn, thawed

1 large onion, chopped (about 1 cup)

4 cloves garlic, minced

1 can (about 14½ ounces) diced tomatoes with green chiles

¼ cup chopped fresh cilantro leaves

1 teaspoon chili powder

2 pounds boneless pork shoulder, cut into 1-inch pieces

1. Stir the broth, sweet potatoes, peppers, corn, onion, garlic, tomatoes, cilantro, chili powder and pork in a 4½- to 5-quart slow cooker.

2. Cover and cook on LOW for 7 to 8 hours* or until the pork is fork-tender.

Makes 8 servings

Or on HIGH for 4 to 5 hours.

Prep Time: 20 minutes
Cook Time: 7 hours
Total Time: 7 hours 20 minutes

zesty chicken & vegetable soup

½ pound boneless skinless chicken breasts, cut into very thin strips

1 to 2 tablespoons FRANK'S® REDHOT® Original Cayenne Pepper Sauce

4 cups chicken broth

1 package (16 ounces) frozen stir-fry vegetables

1 cup angel hair pasta or fine egg noodles, broken into 2-inch lengths

1 green onion, thinly sliced

1. Combine chicken and Frank's RedHot Sauce in medium bowl; set aside.

2. Heat broth to boiling in large saucepan over medium-high heat. Add vegetables and pasta; return to boiling. Cook 2 minutes. Stir in chicken mixture and green onion. Cook 1 minute or until chicken is no longer pink. *Makes 4 to 6 servings*

Tip: For a change of pace, substitute 6 prepared frozen pot stickers for the pasta. Add to broth in step 2 and boil until tender.

slow-cooked panama pork stew

sensational salads

tuna & bow tie salad

8 ounces whole grain or regular bow tie pasta

6 tablespoons **HELLMANN'S®** or **BEST FOODS®** Light Mayonnaise

2 tablespoons red wine vinegar

2 tablespoons chopped fresh basil leaves or 1 teaspoon dried basil, crushed

1 clove garlic, finely chopped

¼ teaspoon ground black pepper

2 cans (6 ounces each) tuna, drained and flaked

1 package (9 ounces) frozen green beans, thawed

2 cups cherry tomatoes, quartered OR grape tomatoes, halved

⅓ cup chopped red onion

1. Cook bow ties according to package directions; drain and rinse with cold water until completely cool.

2. Combine Hellmann's® or Best Foods® Light Mayonnaise, vinegar, basil, garlic and pepper in large bowl.

3. Add remaining ingredients; toss well. Chill, if desired.   *Makes 4 servings*

Variation: Also terrific with Hellmann's® or Best Foods® Low Fat Mayonnaise Dressing.

Prep Time: 15 minutes
Cook Time: 20 minutes

crunchy mexican side salad

3 cups romaine and iceberg
lettuce blend

½ cup grape tomatoes, halved

½ cup peeled and diced jicama

¼ cup **B&G®** Sliced Ripe Olives

¼ cup **ORTEGA®** Sliced
Jalapeños, quartered

2 tablespoons **ORTEGA®**
Taco Sauce

1 tablespoon vegetable oil

⅛ teaspoon salt

Crushed **ORTEGA®**
Taco Shells (optional)

Toss together lettuce, tomatoes, jicama, olives and jalapeños in large bowl.

Combine taco sauce, oil and salt in small bowl. Stir with a fork until blended.

Pour dressing over salad; toss gently to coat. Top with taco shells, if desired.

Makes 4 servings (1 cup each)

Note: Ortega® Sliced Jalapeños are available in a 12-ounce jar. They are pickled, adding great flavor and crunch to this salad.

couscous & roasted vegetable salad

1 (10-ounce) package couscous

1 medium eggplant, peeled,
seeded and chopped into
1-inch pieces

1 red bell pepper, cut into
1-inch pieces

1 yellow bell pepper, cut into
1-inch pieces

3 cloves garlic, minced

5 tablespoons olive oil, divided

⅓ cup red wine vinegar

¼ cup chopped fresh basil *or*
4 teaspoons dried basil

¼ teaspoon black pepper

4 ounces feta cheese, crumbled

Prepare couscous according to package directions. Fluff; cool 10 minutes.

Heat oven to broil. In large bowl, toss eggplant, bell peppers and garlic with 2 tablespoons oil until thoroughly coated. Spread out vegetables on 15×10-inch pan. Broil on top rack 4 to 6 minutes or until eggplant is evenly browned, stirring often.

In large bowl, combine remaining 3 tablespoons oil, vinegar, basil and black pepper. Add couscous and vegetables; toss. Chill 2 hours or overnight. Stir in cheese just before serving.

Makes 8 (1-cup) servings

Favorite recipe from **North Dakota Wheat Commission**

crunchy mexican side salad

pesto rice salad

2 cups MINUTE® White Rice, uncooked

1 package (7 ounces) basil pesto sauce

1 cup cherry tomatoes, halved

8 ounces whole-milk mozzarella cheese, cut into ½-inch cubes

⅓ cup Parmesan cheese, shredded

Toasted pine nuts (optional)

Prepare rice according to package directions. Place in large bowl. Let stand 10 minutes.

Add pesto sauce; mix well. Gently stir in tomatoes and cheese.

Serve warm or cover and refrigerate until ready to serve. Sprinkle with pine nuts, if desired. *Makes 6 servings*

Tip: To toast pine nuts, spread in single layer in heavy-bottomed skillet. Cook over medium heat 1 to 2 minutes, stirring frequently, until nuts are lightly browned. Remove from skillet immediately. Cool before using.

Tip: For a heartier meal, add 1 package (6 ounces) grilled chicken breast strips to the prepared salad.

three-bean salad

1 (15½-ounce) can red kidney beans

1 (14½-ounce) can cut green beans

1 (14½-ounce) can yellow wax beans

1 green bell pepper, seeded and chopped

1 medium onion, chopped

2 ribs celery, sliced

¾ cup cider vinegar

⅓ cup FILIPPO BERIO® Olive Oil

2 tablespoons sugar

Salt and freshly ground black pepper

Rinse and drain kidney beans; drain green and wax beans. In large bowl, combine beans, bell pepper, onion and celery. In small bowl, whisk together vinegar, olive oil and sugar. Pour over bean mixture; toss until lightly coated. Cover; refrigerate several hours or overnight before serving. Season to taste with salt and black pepper. Store salad, covered, in refrigerator up to 1 week. *Makes 10 to 12 servings*

pesto rice salad

festive cranberry-pineapple salad

1 can (20 ounces) crushed pineapple, undrained

2 packages (4-serving size each) or 1 package (8-serving size) JELL-O® Raspberry Flavor Gelatin

1 can (16 ounces) whole berry cranberry sauce

1 medium apple, chopped

⅔ cup chopped PLANTERS® Walnuts

Apple slices (optional)

DRAIN pineapple, reserving liquid in 1-quart liquid measuring cup. Add enough cold water to reserved liquid to measure 3 cups; pour into large saucepan. Bring to boil; remove from heat. Add gelatin; stir at least 2 minutes until completely dissolved. Add cranberry sauce; stir until well blended. (Note: Due to the presence of whole berries in the cranberry sauce, the gelatin mixture will not be smooth.) Pour into large bowl. Refrigerate 1½ hours or until slightly thickened (consistency of unbeaten egg whites).

STIR in pineapple, chopped apple and walnuts; stir gently until well blended. Pour into medium serving bowl.

REFRIGERATE 4 hours or until firm. Garnish with apple slices just before serving, if desired. Store leftover gelatin in refrigerator.   *Makes 14 servings (½ cup each)*

Molded Cranberry-Pineapple Salad: To serve as a molded salad, substitute a 6-cup mold for the serving bowl. Also, use 1 can (8¼ ounces) crushed pineapple, ⅓ cup chopped PLANTERS® Walnuts and add enough cold water to the reserved pineapple liquid to measure 2 cups.

Prep Time: 10 minutes
Total Time: 5 hours 40 minutes (includes refrigerating)

tip: *Fresh or frozen pineapple should not be substituted for canned pineapple in recipes with gelatin, as both contain an enzyme which prevents the gelatin mixture from setting. This enzyme is eliminated by the heat in the canning process, so canned pineapple does not cause any problem in gelatin recipes.*

festive cranberry-pineapple salad

mandarin steak salad

⅓ cup FRENCH'S® Spicy
    Brown Mustard

2 tablespoons teriyaki sauce

1 tablespoon sugar

½ teaspoon garlic powder

½ teaspoon ground ginger

1 can (11 ounces) mandarin
    oranges, *reserve ¼ cup liquid*

1 pound boneless sirloin steak
    (1 inch thick)

8 cups mixed salad greens,
    washed and torn

2 green onions, thinly shredded

⅓ cup dry roasted peanuts,
    chopped

1. Combine mustard, teriyaki sauce, sugar, garlic powder and ginger in small bowl. Stir in reserved mandarin orange liquid. Pour *½ cup* dressing into serving bowl.

2. Brush remaining dressing on steak. Broil or grill steak 10 minutes or until desired doneness. Let stand 5 minutes.

3. Thinly slice steak. Serve over salad greens. Top with oranges, green onions and peanuts. Drizzle with reserved dressing. *Makes 4 servings*

Prep Time: 10 minutes
Cook Time: 10 minutes

italian peasant salad

1 (6.9-ounce) package
    RICE-A-RONI®
    Chicken Flavor

2 tablespoons vegetable oil

1 (16-ounce) can cannellini
    beans, Great Northern
    beans or navy beans,
    rinsed and drained

2 cups chopped cooked chicken

2 medium tomatoes, chopped

1 cup frozen or canned peas,
    drained

½ cup Italian dressing

1 teaspoon dried basil *or*
    ½ teaspoon dried
    rosemary leaves, crushed

1. In large skillet over medium heat, sauté rice-vermicelli mix with oil until vermicelli is golden brown.

2. Slowly stir in 2½ cups water and Special Seasonings; bring to a boil. Reduce heat to low. Cover; simmer 15 to 20 minutes or until rice is tender. Cool 10 minutes.

3. In large bowl, combine rice mixture, beans, chicken, tomatoes, peas, Italian dressing and basil. Cover; chill 1 hour before serving. *Makes 6 servings*

Prep Time: 10 minutes
Cook Time: 25 minutes

mandarin steak salad

border black bean chicken salad

4 TYSON® Trimmed & Ready™ Fresh Boneless Skinless Chicken Breasts

2 tablespoons olive oil

1 garlic clove, minced

½ jalapeño pepper, finely chopped

¾ teaspoon salt

1 cup peeled and seeded cucumber cubes

1 cup red bell pepper strips

1 cup chopped fresh tomato

½ cup chopped red onion

4 cups chopped romaine lettuce

1 can (15 ounces) black beans, rinsed and drained

Dressing

⅓ cup tomato vegetable juice

2 tablespoons fresh lime juice

2 tablespoons olive oil

½ teaspoon ground cumin

½ teaspoon salt

1. Prepare dressing: In small bowl, mix together tomato vegetable juice, lime juice, olive oil, cumin and salt.

2. Cut chicken into 2-inch strips. Wash hands.

3. In large skillet, heat olive oil over medium heat. Add chicken and stir-fry about 2 minutes or until internal juices of chicken run clear. (Or insert instant-read meat thermometer into thickest part of chicken. Temperature should read 180°F.) Add garlic, jalapeño pepper and salt; stir-fry 30 seconds. Remove chicken mixture from skillet and place in large salad bowl.

4. Add cucumber, bell pepper, tomato, onion, lettuce and black beans to chicken in bowl. Add dressing to skillet and heat over medium heat until slightly warm. Pour warm dressing over salad ingredients; toss to coat. Refrigerate leftovers immediately.

Makes 4 servings

Serving Suggestion: Sprinkle with chopped pecans and garnish with a tomato rose and parsley.

Prep Time: 10 minutes
Cook Time: 5 minutes

springtime spinach salad

8 ounces fresh DOLE®
Asparagus Spears or
1 package (10 ounces)
frozen asparagus tips

¼ cup water

1 package (6 ounces) DOLE®
Baby Spinach or Spinach
and Leaf Salad Blends

1½ cups DOLE® Frozen Sliced
Strawberries, partially
thawed

½ cup julienne-sliced red onion

½ cup Raspberry Dressing
(*recipe follows*) or red
wine and vinegar dressing

⅔ cup crumbled feta or blue
cheese

BREAK off woody ends of asparagus (the bottom 1 to 1½ inches) and discard. Cut asparagus into 1-inch lengths. Place in a microwavable dish with water. Microwave on HIGH power for 3 minutes. Immediately rinse asparagus under cold water for 1 minute; drain well.

PLACE salad blend, drained asparagus, strawberries and onion in a large bowl.

POUR dressing over salad; toss to evenly coat. Sprinkle cheese over salad.

Makes 6 side-dish servings

Prep Time: 15 minutes

raspberry dressing

¾ cup DOLE® Frozen
Raspberries, thawed

⅓ to ½ cup orange juice

⅓ cup olive oil

1 tablespoon honey

¼ teaspoon salt

PLACE raspberries, orange juice, olive oil, honey and salt in blender or food processor container. Cover; blend until smooth.

Makes 1¼ cups

springtime spinach salad

german potato salad

10 medium potatoes
1¾ cups SWANSON® Beef Broth
  (Regular, Lower Sodium or
  Certified Organic)
¼ cup cider vinegar
¼ cup all-purpose flour
3 tablespoons sugar

½ teaspoon celery seed
⅛ teaspoon ground black pepper
1 medium onion, chopped
  (about ½ cup)
3 tablespoons chopped fresh
  parsley

1. Place the potatoes into a 4-quart saucepan. Add water to cover. Heat over high heat to a boil. Reduce the heat to low. Cook for 20 minutes or until the potatoes are tender. Drain. Let cool and cut in cubes. Place the potatoes into a large bowl.

2. Stir the broth, vinegar, flour, sugar, celery seed and black pepper in the saucepan. Stir in the onion. Cook and stir over medium-high heat until the mixture boils and thickens. Reduce the heat to low. Cook for 5 minutes or until the onion is tender.

3. Add the parsley and broth mixture to the potatoes and stir to coat. Serve warm.

Makes 12 servings

Kitchen Tip: You can let this dish stand for a few minutes before serving. The dressing will soak into the warm potatoes—delicious!

Prep Time: 15 minutes
Cook Time: 30 minutes
Total Time: 45 minutes

classic waldorf salad

½ cup HELLMANN'S® or
  BEST FOODS® Real
  Mayonnaise
1 tablespoon sugar
1 tablespoon lemon juice
⅛ teaspoon salt

3 medium red apples, cored
  and diced
1 cup chopped celery
¼ cup raisins (optional)
½ cup chopped walnuts

1. In medium bowl blend mayonnaise, sugar, lemon juice and salt. Stir in apples, celery and raisins. Cover and chill to blend flavors. Just before serving, sprinkle with walnuts.

Makes about 8 servings

Prep Time: 20 minutes
Chill Time: 30 minutes

german potato salad

easy tossed niçoise with garlic and cheese dressing

1½ pounds steamed red potatoes, cut into small chunks

1 package (10 ounces) frozen Italian green beans, thawed and drained

¾ cup niçoise or pitted ripe olives, sliced

½ red onion, slivered

½ red bell pepper, slivered

½ green bell pepper, slivered

¼ cup coarsely chopped green onions, including tops

1½ cups Garlic and Cheese Dressing (recipe follows)

1 (6.4-ounce) STARKIST Flavor Fresh Pouch® Tuna (Albacore)

½ cup minced fresh parsley

Whole romaine leaves, washed and dried

Freshly ground black pepper (optional)

Grated Parmesan cheese (optional)

In large bowl, combine potatoes, beans, olives, red onion, bell peppers and green onions; toss with Garlic and Cheese Dressing. Refrigerate. Just before serving, add tuna and parsley. Line plates with lettuce; spoon salad onto leaves. Serve with black pepper and cheese, if desired.

Makes 6 to 8 servings

Prep Time: 15 minutes

garlic and cheese dressing

¼ cup wine vinegar

2 tablespoons lemon juice

1 tablespoon Dijon-style mustard

1 to 2 cloves garlic, minced or pressed

Salt and black pepper to taste

1 cup olive oil

½ cup grated Parmesan cheese

In small bowl, whisk together vinegar, lemon juice, mustard, garlic, salt and pepper. Slowly add olive oil, whisking until all oil is added and dressing is thickened. Stir in cheese.

easy tossed niçoise with garlic and cheese dressing

gazpacho steak salad

1 pound beef shoulder steak *or*
1 pound beef top round
steak, cut 1 inch thick

1 can (5½ ounces) spicy 100%
vegetable juice

8 cups mixed greens *or* 1 package
(10 ounces) romaine and leaf
lettuce mixture

1 cup baby pear tomatoes,
halved

1 cup cucumber, cut in half
lengthwise, then into
thin slices

1 cup chopped green bell pepper

Salt and pepper

Crunchy Tortilla Strips
(recipe follows)

Gazpacho Dressing

1 can (5½ ounces) spicy 100%
vegetable juice

½ cup chopped tomato

¼ cup finely chopped green bell
pepper

1 tablespoon red wine vinegar

1 tablespoon chopped cilantro

2 teaspoons olive oil

1 clove garlic, minced

1. Place beef steak and 1 can vegetable juice in food-safe plastic bag; turn steak to coat. Close bag securely and marinate in refrigerator 6 hours or as long as overnight.

2. Combine dressing ingredients; refrigerate. Combine greens, baby pear tomatoes, cucumber and 1 cup green bell pepper; refrigerate.

3. Remove steak from marinade; discard marinade. Place steak on grid over medium, ash-covered coals. Grill shoulder steak, uncovered, 16 to 20 minutes for medium rare (145°F) to medium (160°F) doneness (top round steak 16 to 18 minutes for medium rare doneness; do not overcook), turning occasionally. Carve steak across the grain into thin slices. Season with salt and pepper, as desired.

4. Meanwhile, prepare Crunchy Tortilla Strips. Add steak to salad mixture. Drizzle with dressing and top with tortilla strips. *Makes 4 servings*

Crunchy Tortilla Strips: Heat oven to 400°F. Cut 2 corn tortillas in half, then cut crosswise into ¼-inch-wide strips. Place strips in single layer on baking sheet. Bake 4 to 8 minutes or until crisp.

Cook's Tip: To prepare on gas grill, preheat grill according to manufacturer's directions for medium heat. Grill shoulder steak, covered, 15 to 19 minutes for medium rare to medium doneness (top round steak 16 to 19 minutes for medium rare doneness; do not overcook), turning occasionally.

Prep and Cook Time: 30 minutes
Marinate Time: 6 hours or overnight

Favorite recipe from **Courtesy The Beef Checkoff**

gazpacho steak salad

watergate salad

1 package (4-serving size) instant
  pistachio pudding and
  pie filling
1 can (20 ounces) DOLE®
  Crushed Pineapple,
  undrained

1 cup miniature marshmallows
½ cup chopped pecans
1½ cups (½ of 8-ounce tub)
  thawed whipped topping

MIX dry pudding mix, pineapple, marshmallows and pecans in large bowl until well blended. Gently stir in whipped topping; cover.

REFRIGERATE 1 hour or until ready to serve.   *Makes 8 servings*

Prep Time: 15 minutes
Refrigerate Time: 1 hour

asian salmon salad

1 medium orange
1 pound salmon fillet, cut into
  4 strips
½ cup WISH-BONE® Italian
  Dressing, divided
3 tablespoons SKIPPY®
  Creamy Peanut Butter

1 teaspoon finely grated fresh
  ginger OR ¼ teaspoon
  ground ginger
8 cups baby spinach leaves
1 small red onion, thinly sliced
1 cup shelled and cooked
  edamame
⅓ cup sliced almonds, toasted

1. Preheat oven to 400°F. From the orange, grate enough peel to measure 2 teaspoons; set aside. Peel and section orange; reserve. Arrange salmon in 8-inch glass baking dish; set aside.

2. Combine ¼ cup Wish-Bone® Italian Dressing, Skippy® Creamy Peanut Butter, orange peel and ginger in small bowl. Evenly spread dressing mixture on salmon. Bake 12 minutes or until salmon flakes with a fork.

3. Meanwhile, arrange spinach and onion on serving platter. Top with orange and edamame, then arrange salmon and almonds. Just before serving, drizzle with remaining ¼ cup dressing.   *Makes 4 servings*

Prep Time: 15 minutes
Cook Time: 12 minutes

watergate salad

grilled potato salad

1 envelope LIPTON®
RECIPE SECRETS®
Onion Soup Mix*

⅓ cup olive oil

2 tablespoons red wine vinegar

1 clove garlic, finely chopped

2 pounds small red or
all-purpose potatoes,
cut into 1-inch cubes

1 tablespoon chopped fresh basil
leaves or 1 teaspoon dried
basil leaves, crushed

Freshly ground black pepper

*Also terrific with LIPTON® RECIPE
SECRETS® Onion Mushroom or Golden
Onion Soup Mix.

1. In large bowl, blend soup mix, oil, vinegar and garlic; stir in potatoes.

2. Grease 30×18-inch sheet of heavy-duty aluminum foil; top with potato mixture. Wrap foil loosely around mixture, sealing edges airtight with double fold. Place on another sheet of 30×18-inch foil; seal edges airtight with double fold in opposite direction.

3. Grill, shaking package occasionally and turning package once, 40 minutes or until potatoes are tender. Spoon into serving bowl and toss with basil and pepper. Serve slightly warm or at room temperature. *Makes 4 servings*

Oven Method: Preheat oven to 450°F. Prepare foil packet as above. Place in large baking pan on bottom rack and bake, turning packet once, 40 minutes or until potatoes are tender. Toss and serve as above.

santa fe salad

2 cups cooked brown rice, cooled

1 can (16 ounces) black beans
or pinto beans, rinsed and
drained

1 can (15 ounces) whole kernel
corn, drained

¼ cup minced onion

¼ cup white vinegar

2 tablespoons vegetable oil

2 tablespoons snipped cilantro

2 jalapeño peppers, minced

2 teaspoons chili powder

1 teaspoon salt

Combine rice, beans, corn and onion in medium bowl. Combine vinegar, oil, cilantro, peppers, chili powder and salt in small jar with lid; shake well. Pour over rice mixture; toss lightly. Cover and chill 2 to 3 hours so flavors will blend. Stir before serving. *Makes 4 servings*

Favorite recipe from **USA Rice**

grilled potato salad

antipasto salad

1 package **HILLSHIRE FARM**® Smoked Sausage

6 cups mixed salad greens

2 cups red and yellow grape tomatoes

1 tomato, cut into wedges

1 small cucumber, sliced

1 cup small cauliflower florets

¾ cup pitted ripe black olives

⅔ cup Italian salad dressing

1 package (4 ounces) crumbled feta cheese, about 1 cup

2 green onions, sliced

1. Cut sausage in ½-inch slices. Heat a large nonstick skillet over medium-high heat for 3 minutes. Cook sausage 2 minutes on each side or until lightly browned; remove from pan and drain on paper towels.

2. Arrange salad greens on large platter. Place cooked sausage in center of platter in a row. Arrange tomatoes, cucumber, cauliflower and olives in rows on either side of the sausage.

3. Pour salad dressing over vegetables and sausage. Sprinkle with feta cheese and green onions. *Makes 4 servings*

belgioioso® fresh mozzarella and pepper salad

2 red bell peppers

2 yellow bell peppers

2 balls **BELGIOIOSO**® Fresh Mozzarella, sliced

½ cup extra-virgin olive oil

½ teaspoon salt

¼ teaspoon ground pepper

4 fresh basil leaves, cut into thin pieces

Preheat broiler. Place peppers under broiler until blackened all over, about 12 to 15 minutes. Let cool in paper bag. Remove stems, skins and seeds. Cut into ¼-inch strips.

On a platter, arrange a row of alternating colored pepper strips, slightly overlapping. Arrange an overlapping row of Belgioioso Fresh Mozzarella next to them. Continue alternating until all are used. Drizzle oil over the peppers and cheese, and sprinkle with salt, pepper and basil. Serve immediately. *Makes 4 servings*

antipasto salad

mediterranean chop salad

3 stalks celery, sliced (about 1½ cups) or 1 cup sliced fennel

1 cup chopped roasted red or yellow pepper

1 large seedless cucumber, peeled and chopped (about 1⅔ cups)

½ cup chopped pitted ripe olives

½ cup prepared balsamic vinaigrette salad dressing

1 package (12 ounces) hearts of romaine, chopped (about 8 cups)

1 box (5.5 ounces) **PEPPERIDGE FARM®** Seasoned Croutons (your favorite variety)

Freshly ground black pepper

Parmesan cheese shavings

1. Stir the celery, pepper, cucumber, olives and dressing in a large serving bowl. Cover and refrigerate until serving time.

2. Add the lettuce and croutons to the dressing mixture just before serving and toss to coat. Season with the black pepper. Top with the cheese.   *Makes 8 servings*

Prep Time: 25 minutes
Total Time: 25 minutes

strawberry banana salad

1½ cups boiling water

1 package (8-serving size) or 2 packages (4-serving size each) JELL-O® Brand Strawberry or Strawberry Banana Flavor Sugar Free Low Calorie Gelatin

2 cups cold water

1 cup chopped strawberries

1 banana, sliced

STIR boiling water into gelatin in large bowl at least 2 minutes until completely dissolved. Stir in cold water. Refrigerate about 1½ hours or until thickened (spoon drawn through leaves definite impression).

STIR in strawberries and banana. Pour into 5-cup mold that has been sprayed with nonstick cooking spray.

REFRIGERATE 4 hours or until firm. Unmold. Store leftover gelatin mold in refrigerator.   *Makes 10 (½-cup) servings*

Prep Time: 15 minutes
Refrigerate Time: 5½ hours

mediterranean chop salad

main
dishes

lipton® onion burgers with creamy salsa & spanish rice

1 envelope LIPTON®
   RECIPE SECRETS®
   Onion Soup Mix
2 pounds lean ground beef
½ cup water
½ cup HELLMANN'S® or
   BEST FOODS® Real
   Mayonnaise

½ cup chunky salsa, drained
   if desired
8 whole wheat or regular
   hamburger buns
1 package KNORR® FIESTA
   SIDES™–Spanish Rice,
   prepared according to
   package directions

1. Combine soup mix, ground beef and water in large bowl; shape into 8 patties. Grill or broil until done.

2. Meanwhile, combine Hellmann's® or Best Foods® Real Mayonnaise with salsa in small bowl.

3. Arrange onion burgers on buns, then top with creamy salsa. Serve with hot Knorr® Fiesta Sides™–Spanish Rice.
Makes 8 servings

Tip: Also delicious with Knorr® Rice Sides™–Beef or Mushroom.

Prep Time: 10 minutes
Cook Time: 10 minutes

shrimp tostadas

1 pound cooked shrimp, peeled and deveined

1 can (14½ ounces) diced tomatoes, drained

1 cup chopped white onion

1 can (4 ounces) ORTEGA® Fire-Roasted Diced Green Chiles

¼ cup chopped fresh cilantro

3 tablespoons vegetable oil

3 tablespoons lime juice

1 can (16 ounces) ORTEGA® Refried Beans, warmed

1 package (10-count) ORTEGA® Tostada Shells, warmed

2½ cups shredded lettuce

Combine shrimp, tomatoes, onions, chiles, cilantro, oil and lime juice in medium bowl; cover.

Spread about 2 tablespoons beans on each tostada shell. Top with ¼ cup lettuce and ½ cup shrimp mixture.   *Makes 10 servings*

Tip: The shrimp mixture may be prepared in advance and refrigerated.

Tip: To warm the tostada shells, place them on a baking sheet; bake 5 to 10 minutes or until warmed.

chicken piccata

4 ounces dried fettuccini or linguine

¼ cup all-purpose flour

½ teaspoon lemon pepper seasoning

2 teaspoons HERB-OX® chicken flavored bouillon, divided

4 boneless, skinless chicken breasts (1 to 1¼ pounds), pounded to ⅛-inch thickness

2 tablespoons olive oil

⅓ cup dry white wine

3 tablespoons lemon juice

2 tablespoons water

2 tablespoons chopped fresh parsley

1 tablespoon capers, drained and rinsed

Cook pasta in bouillon-seasoned water. Meanwhile, in bowl, stir together flour, lemon pepper and ½ teaspoon bouillon. Dip chicken in flour mixture to coat. In skillet, cook chicken in oil over medium-high heat for 2 to 3 minutes per side or until golden brown and no longer pink. Remove chicken from pan; keep warm. For sauce, add wine, lemon juice, water and remaining bouillon to skillet. Bring mixture to a boil. Simmer for 2 minutes. Stir in parsley and capers. Serve chicken over pasta and top with sauce.

Makes 4 servings

shrimp tostada

cranberry glazed chicken with orange-berry couscous

½ teaspoon salt

½ teaspoon rubbed dried sage, divided

¼ teaspoon black pepper

4 boneless skinless chicken breasts

2 tablespoons canola oil

1 can (16 ounces) jellied cranberry sauce

¼ cup packed brown sugar

¼ cup orange juice

2 tablespoons coarse ground mustard

1 teaspoon grated orange peel

Orange-Berry Couscous (recipe follows)

In a small bowl, mix together salt, ¼ teaspoon dried sage and pepper. Sprinkle over chicken pieces. In nonstick skillet, heat oil to medium-high heat. Add chicken; cook about 6 to 8 minutes per side or until no longer pink in center. Remove chicken to platter; keep warm. Drain excess oil from pan. To same pan, add cranberry sauce, brown sugar, orange juice, mustard, orange peel and remaining sage. Heat, stirring, to boiling; reduce heat and simmer about 5 minutes until cranberry sauce melts and glaze thickens slightly. Return chicken to pan and heat, uncovered, about 3 minutes, turning chicken several times to glaze. Place Orange-Berry Couscous on serving plate. Top with chicken breasts and drizzle cranberry glaze over chicken. Pass remaining sauce.

Makes 4 servings

Orange-Berry Couscous: In a saucepan, place 1 cup chicken broth and heat to boiling. Stir in ¾ cup wheat couscous; cover and remove from heat. Let stand 5 minutes or until liquid is absorbed. Stir in ½ cup dried cranberries and 1 teaspoon grated orange peel. Makes about 2¼ cups.

Favorite recipe from **Delmarva Poultry Industry, Inc.**

cranberry glazed chicken with orange-berry couscous

blackened catfish with creole vegetables

⅔ cup **CATTLEMEN'S®**
  Authentic Smoke House
  Barbecue Sauce or
  CATTLEMEN'S®
  Award Winning Classic
  Barbecue Sauce

⅓ cup **FRANK'S® REDHOT®**
  Original Cayenne
  Pepper Sauce

2 tablespoons Southwest
  chile seasoning blend or
  Cajun blend seasoning

1 tablespoon olive oil

4 skinless catfish or sea bass fillets
  (1½ pounds)

Salt and pepper to taste

Creole Vegetables
  (recipe follows)

1. Combine barbecue sauce, Frank's RedHot Sauce, seasoning blend and oil. Reserve ½ cup mixture for Creole Vegetables.

2. Season fish with salt and pepper to taste. Baste fish with remaining barbecue mixture.

3. Cook fish on a well-greased grill over medium direct heat 5 minutes per side until fish is opaque in center, turning once. Serve with Creole Vegetables.

Makes 4 servings

Prep Time: 20 minutes
Cook Time: 15 minutes

creole vegetables

1 red, green or orange bell
  pepper, cut into quarters

1 large green zucchini or
  summer squash, cut in half
  crosswise, then lengthwise
  into thick slices

1 large white onion, sliced
  ½ inch thick

Vegetable cooking spray

Arrange vegetables on skewers. Coat vegetables with cooking spray. Grill vegetables over medium direct heat until lightly charred and tender, basting often with reserved ½ cup barbecue sauce mixture.

Makes 4 servings

chicken gyros with yogurt dill sauce

Chicken Gyros

1 bag (6 ounces) TYSON®
  Grilled & Ready
  Refrigerated Fully Cooked
  Grilled Chicken Breast Strips
1 teaspoon dried oregano
1 teaspoon chopped fresh dill
  Salt and black pepper, to taste
2 tablespoons olive oil, divided
2 medium onions, thinly sliced

1 tablespoon fresh lemon juice
4 pita bread rounds, heated

Yogurt Dill Sauce

1 cup fat-free plain yogurt
2 tablespoons chopped fresh dill
1 large garlic clove, minced
1 teaspoon fresh lemon juice
  Salt and black pepper, to taste

1. Place chicken in medium bowl. Sprinkle with oregano, 1 teaspoon dill, salt and pepper. Toss to coat. Heat 1 tablespoon oil in heavy large skillet over medium-high heat. Add chicken; cook and stir until brown and heated through, about 2 minutes. Transfer to plate.

2. Add remaining 1 tablespoon oil to skillet. Add onions; cook and stir until beginning to brown, about 10 minutes. Return chicken and any juices to skillet. Add 1 tablespoon lemon juice. Stir until heated through, about 2 minutes.

3. To make sauce, stir yogurt, 2 tablespoons dill, garlic and 1 teaspoon lemon juice in small bowl to blend. Season with salt and pepper, to taste.

4. Arrange pita rounds on plates. Top with chicken mixture. Spoon yogurt sauce over chicken. Serve, passing extra sauce separately. Refrigerate leftovers immediately.

Makes 4 servings

Prep Time: 5 minutes
Cook Time: 15 minutes
Total Time: 20 minutes

tip: *If you purchase a bunch of fresh dill for this recipe, you will end up with quite a bit left over. For short-term storage, place the dill stems in water, cover the leaves loosely with a plastic bag or plastic wrap and store in the refrigerator (where it will last several days).*

chicken gyro with yogurt dill sauce

braised short ribs with red wine tomato sauce

4 pounds beef short ribs, cut into serving-sized pieces

2⅔ cups PREGO® Fresh Mushroom Italian Sauce

1 cup dry red wine

1 bag fresh or frozen whole baby carrots

1 large onion, chopped (about 1 cup)

Hot cooked rice

1. Season the ribs as desired.

2. Stir the Italian sauce, wine, carrots and onion in a 3½-quart slow cooker. Add the ribs and turn to coat.

3. Cover and cook on LOW for 7 to 8 hours* or until the ribs are fork-tender. Serve with the rice. *Makes 8 servings*

Or on HIGH for 4 to 5 hours.

pesto-topped halibut

⅓ cup HELLMANN'S® or BEST FOODS® Mayonnaise Dressing with Extra Virgin Olive Oil

1 cup loosely packed fresh basil leaves

¼ cup pine nuts or walnuts

¼ cup grated Parmesan cheese

1 clove garlic

4 halibut or cod fillets (about 1 pound)

1. Preheat oven to 425°F. Lightly grease baking sheet; set aside.

2. In food processor or blender, process all ingredients except halibut until well blended. Evenly spread on halibut.

3. Bake 15 minutes or until halibut flakes with a fork. *Makes 4 servings*

Prep Time: 10 minutes
Cook Time: 15 minutes

braised short ribs with red wine tomato sauce

honey mustard glazed salmon with tropical fruit salsa

3 tablespoons spicy brown mustard

2 tablespoons honey

¾ teaspoon salt, divided

¼ teaspoon hot pepper sauce

1 can (15.25 ounces) DOLE® Tropical Fruit, drained and diced

1 avocado, peeled and diced

⅓ cup diced red bell pepper

¼ cup chopped DOLE® Red Onion

1 tablespoon lime juice

1⅓ pounds salmon fillets

STIR together mustard, honey, ½ teaspoon salt and hot pepper sauce in small bowl.

COMBINE tropical fruit, avocado, bell pepper, onion, lime juice and remaining ¼ teaspoon salt. Cover; refrigerate salsa until ready to serve.

GRILL or broil salmon 4 to 5 minutes, brushing with honey-mustard glaze; turn over. Grill or broil 4 to 5 minutes more or until desired doneness, brushing with remaining glaze. Serve salmon with tropical fruit salsa. *Makes 4 servings*

deep dish chicken pot pie

1 pound boneless, skinless chicken breasts, cut into 1-inch pieces

¼ cup KRAFT® Light Zesty Italian Reduced Fat Dressing

4 ounces (½ of 8-ounce package) PHILADELPHIA® Neufchâtel Cheese, cubed

2 tablespoons all-purpose flour

½ cup fat-free reduced-sodium chicken broth

1 package (10 ounces) frozen mixed vegetables, thawed

1 refrigerated pie crust (½ of 15-ounce package)

HEAT oven to 375°F. Cook chicken in dressing in large skillet on medium heat 2 minutes. Add Neufchâtel cheese; cook and stir until melted. Add flour; mix well. Add broth and vegetables; simmer 5 minutes.

POUR mixture into deep-dish 10-inch pie plate. Arrange pie crust over filling; flute edges. Cut 4 slits in crust to allow steam to escape.

BAKE 30 minutes or until crust is golden brown. *Makes 6 servings*

honey mustard glazed salmon with tropical fruit salsa

meatball hero sandwiches

1 pound lean ground beef	4 Italian rolls, (about 6 inches long each), halved lengthwise
½ cup Italian seasoned dry bread crumbs	
1 egg	½ cup shredded mozzarella cheese (about 2 ounces)
1 jar (1 pound 10 ounces) RAGÚ® Old World Style® or Chunky Pasta Sauce	

1. Combine ground beef, bread crumbs and egg in medium bowl; shape into 12 meatballs.

2. Bring Pasta Sauce to a boil in 3-quart saucepan over medium-high heat. Gently stir in uncooked meatballs.

3. Reduce heat to low and simmer covered, stirring occasionally, 20 minutes or until meatballs are done. Serve meatballs and sauce in rolls and top with cheese.

Makes 4 servings

Tip: Use ground turkey to make turkey meatballs.

Prep Time: 10 minutes
Cook Time: 25 minutes

crunchy cajun fish fingers

2⅔ cups FRENCH'S® French Fried Onions	1 teaspoon FRANK'S® REDHOT® Original Cayenne Pepper Sauce
2 teaspoons Cajun spice blend	1 pound catfish or tilapia fillets, cut crosswise into 1-inch strips
2 tablespoons reduced-fat mayonnaise	

1. Mix French Fried Onions and Cajun spice in plastic bag. Crush with hands or rolling pin.

2. Combine mayonnaise and Frank's RedHot Sauce in large bowl. Add fish strips to bowl and toss to coat.

3. Dip coated fish strips into onion crumbs.

4. Bake fish strips on foil-lined baking sheet at 400°F for 15 minutes or until fish flakes with a fork.

Makes 4 servings

meatball hero sandwich

easy shepherd's pie

1½ pounds lean ground beef	1 cup frozen corn niblets, thawed
1 cup chopped onion	1 teaspoon dried thyme leaves
2 cups frozen green beans, thawed	½ teaspoon salt
1 can (14½ ounces) diced tomatoes, drained	1 package SIMPLY POTATOES® Mashed Potatoes
1 jar (12 ounces) beef gravy	

1. Heat oven to 375°F. Spray 2½- to 3-quart casserole baking dish with nonstick cooking spray.

2. In 12-inch skillet cook ground beef and onion until browned; drain grease. Add beans, tomatoes, gravy, corn, thyme and salt. Cook until heated through. Spoon beef mixture into casserole dish. Spread Simply Potatoes® evenly over beef mixture. Bake 30 to 35 minutes or until edges are bubbly. Remove from oven.

3. Heat broiler. Broil casserole 4 to 6 inches from heat, 3 to 5 minutes, until Simply Potatoes® are lightly browned. *Makes 6 servings*

cashew beef

2 tablespoons cooking oil	½ cup carrot slices (½-inch slices)
8 ounces beef (flank steak, skirt steak, top sirloin or filet mignon), cut into strips ¼ inch thick	¼ cup small button mushroom halves
3 tablespoons LEE KUM KEE® Premium Brand, Panda Brand or Choy Sun Oyster Sauce	2 tablespoons LEE KUM KEE® Soy Sauce
	1 green onion, chopped
	2 tablespoons cashews, toasted*
¼ cup *each* red and green bell pepper strips (1-inch strips)	1 tablespoon LEE KUM KEE® Chili Garlic Sauce or Sriracha Chili Sauce
2 stalks celery, cut into ½-inch slices	

Cashews can be toasted in wok or skillet prior to cooking beef.

1. Heat wok or skillet over high heat until hot. Add oil, beef and LEE KUM KEE Oyster Sauce; cook until beef is half done.

2. Add bell peppers, celery, carrots, mushrooms and LEE KUM KEE Soy Sauce; stir-fry until vegetables are crisp-tender. Stir in green onion and cashews. Add LEE KUM KEE Chili Garlic Sauce or Sriracha Chili Sauce for spiciness or use as dipping sauce. *Makes 2 servings*

easy shepherd's pie

beef and broccoli stir-fry

2 cups **MINUTE®** Brown Rice, uncooked

1 pound beef flank steak, cut into strips

2 teaspoons cornstarch

¼ cup orange juice

1 teaspoon ground ginger

1 tablespoon vegetable oil

1 package (10 ounces) frozen broccoli florets, thawed

1 can (8 ounces) sliced water chestnuts, drained

¼ cup reduced-sodium soy sauce

¼ cup dry-roasted peanuts (optional)

Prepare rice according to package directions.

Place steak strips in medium bowl. Sprinkle with cornstarch; toss to coat. Add orange juice and ginger; stir until well blended.

Heat oil in large nonstick skillet over medium-high heat. Add steak mixture; stir-fry 4 to 5 minutes or until steak is cooked through. Reduce heat to medium-low.

Add broccoli, water chestnuts and soy sauce; mix well. Cover; simmer 5 minutes or until thickened, stirring frequently. Serve over rice; sprinkle with peanuts, if desired.

Makes 4 servings

Tip: To make slicing easier, place steak in freezer for 30 minutes to 1 hour before cutting into strips.

prize-winning meatloaf

1½ pounds 90% lean ground beef

1 cup tomato juice or tomato sauce

¾ cup **QUAKER®** Oats (quick or old fashioned, uncooked)

1 egg or 2 egg whites, lightly beaten

¼ cup chopped onion

½ teaspoon salt (optional)

¼ teaspoon black pepper

1. Heat oven to 350°F. Combine beef, tomato juice, oats, egg, onion, salt, if desired, and pepper in large bowl, mixing lightly but thoroughly. Shape into 8×4-inch loaf on rack in broiler pan.

2. Bake 1 hour to medium doneness (160°F) until no longer pink in center and juices show no pink color. Let stand 5 minutes.

Makes 8 servings

Tips: Sprinkle top of baked meatloaf with 1 cup shredded cheese. Return to oven for 3 minutes to melt cheese. Or, spoon heated prepared spaghetti sauce, pizza sauce, barbecue sauce or salsa over each serving.

pineapple teriyaki chicken kabobs

1 can (20 ounces) DOLE®
    Pineapple Chunks

¾ cup prepared teriyaki
    marinade with pineapple
    juice

1 teaspoon Dijon-style mustard

4 boneless, skinless chicken
    breasts, cut into 1-inch
    pieces (1½ to 1¾ pounds)

2 red or green bell peppers,
    cut into 1½-inch pieces

1 zucchini, cut into ½-inch-thick
    slices

12 wooden skewers (12 inches
    long), soaked in water

DRAIN pineapple; reserve 2 tablespoons juice.

COMBINE pineapple juice, teriyaki marinade and mustard. Set aside ¼ cup for grilling. Pour remaining marinade into resealable plastic bag; add chicken pieces, bell peppers and zucchini. Refrigerate and marinate for 30 minutes.

REMOVE chicken and vegetables from plastic bag and discard marinade.

THREAD bell peppers, pineapple chunks, chicken and zucchini onto skewers. Brush with reserved marinade.

GRILL or broil 10 to 15 minutes, turning and brushing occasionally with teriyaki marinade, or until chicken is no longer pink. Discard any remaining marinade.

Makes 4 servings

crusted tilapia florentine

1 egg

2 teaspoons water

1 cup Italian-seasoned dry
    bread crumbs

4 fresh tilapia fillets
    (about 4 ounces each)

2 tablespoons olive oil

2⅔ cups PREGO® Traditional
    Italian Sauce

2 cups frozen chopped spinach

Hot cooked noodles

1. Beat the egg and water with a fork in a shallow dish. Place the bread crumbs on a plate. Dip the fish in the egg mixture, then coat with the bread crumbs.

2. Heat the oil in a 12-inch skillet over medium-high heat. Add the fish and cook for 8 minutes, turning once or until the fish flakes easily when tested with a fork. Remove the fish and keep warm.

3. Stir the Italian sauce and spinach into the skillet. Heat to a boil. Reduce the heat to medium. Cook for 2 minutes or until the mixture is hot. Serve the sauce over the fish. Serve with the noodles.

Makes 4 servings

pineapple teriyaki chicken kabobs

easy santa fe style stuffed peppers

1 cup MINUTE® Brown Rice,
  uncooked

Nonstick cooking spray

1 pound lean ground beef*

1 package (10 ounces) frozen
  whole-kernel corn

1½ cups chunky salsa

4 large red bell peppers, tops
  and seeds removed**

1 cup Colby and Monterey Jack
  cheese, shredded

*Or substitute ground turkey.

**Or substitute green, yellow or orange bell
peppers.

Prepare rice according to package directions.

Preheat oven to 425°F.

Spray large nonstick skillet with nonstick cooking spray. Add beef and brown over medium heat; drain excess fat. Stir in corn, salsa and rice.

Pierce bell peppers with fork or sharp knife; place in baking dish. Fill peppers with meat mixture. Cover with foil.

Bake 20 minutes. Uncover. Sprinkle with cheese before serving.   *Makes 4 servings*

Tip: If softer peppers are desired, reduce the oven temperature to 375°F and cook the filled peppers, covered, for 1 hour.

maple-glazed cornish hens

2 TYSON® Cornish Game Hen
  Twin Packs (4 total), thawed

¼ cup apple juice frozen
  concentrate

¼ cup maple syrup

2 tablespoons finely chopped
  onion

2 teaspoons prepared mustard

1. Heat grill to medium. Cut each hen down backbone and spread flat on cutting board. Rinse hens and pat dry. Combine remaining ingredients in small saucepan. Bring to a boil, stirring occasionally. Cook 5 minutes, stirring occasionally. Remove from heat. Pour half of glaze mixture into small bowl; reserve.

2. Place hens directly over burners or coals on grill. Wash hands. Grill hens, covered, 20 minutes, turning once. Brush hens with remaining glaze. Turn and baste again. Grill, covered, 10 to 15 minutes longer. Brush with glaze; turn and baste again. Grill, covered, 10 to 15 minutes longer or until internal juices of hens run clear. (Or insert instant-read meat thermometer into thickest part of hens. Temperature should read 180°F.) Drizzle with reserved glaze mixture before serving. Refrigerate leftovers immediately.   *Makes 4 servings*

easy santa fe style stuffed peppers

yankee pot roast

1 boneless beef chuck pot roast (arm, shoulder or blade), about 2½ pounds

⅓ cup all-purpose flour

¾ teaspoon salt

¾ teaspoon pepper

1 tablespoon vegetable oil

1 can (14 to 14½ ounces) beef broth

½ cup dry red wine

1½ teaspoons dried thyme leaves, crushed

2 packages (16 ounces *each*) frozen stew vegetable mixture (such as potatoes, carrots, celery and onion)

1. Combine flour, salt and pepper. Lightly coat beef in 2 tablespoons of the flour mixture. Heat oil in large stockpot over medium heat until hot. Place beef pot roast in stockpot; brown evenly. Pour off drippings.

2. Combine beef broth, red wine, thyme and remaining flour mixture; add to stockpot and bring to a boil. Reduce heat; cover tightly and simmer 2 hours. Add vegetables to stockpot; continue simmering 30 to 45 minutes or until pot roast and vegetables are fork-tender.

3. Remove pot roast and vegetables; keep warm. Skim fat from cooking liquid, if necessary.

4. Cut pot roast into bite-size pieces. Serve with vegetables and gravy.

Makes 6 servings

Prep and Cook Time: 3 to 3½ hours

Favorite recipe from **Courtesy The Beef Checkoff**

tip: *Pot roasts from the chuck have more fat, and therefore more flavor, than those from the round. This cut also contains more connective tissue than other roasts (such as rib roasts, top loin or tenderloin), which is why braising (slow cooking in a small amount of liquid) is the best cooking method to achieve flavorful, fork-tender meat.*

family-favorite roast chicken

1 (4½-pound) roasting chicken
¼ teaspoon black pepper
⅛ teaspoon salt
1 medium lemon, washed

4 ounces (½ of 8-ounce package)
  PHILADELPHIA®
  Cream Cheese, softened
1 tablespoon Italian seasoning
½ cup KRAFT® Zesty Italian
  Dressing

HEAT oven to 350°F. Rinse chicken; pat dry with paper towel. Use the tip of a sharp knife to separate the chicken skin from the meat in the chicken breast and tops of the legs. Sprinkle chicken both inside and out with the pepper and salt. Place in 13×9-inch baking dish.

GRATE the lemon; mix the peel with cream cheese and Italian seasoning. Use a small spoon or your fingers to carefully stuff the cream cheese mixture under the chicken skin, pushing the cream cheese mixture carefully toward the legs, being careful to not tear the skin.

CUT the lemon in half; squeeze both halves into small bowl. Add dressing; beat with wire whisk until well blended. Drizzle evenly over chicken. Place the squeezed lemon halves inside the chicken cavity. Insert an ovenproof meat thermometer into thickest part of 1 of the chicken's thighs.

BAKE 1 hour 30 minutes or until chicken is no longer pink in center (165°F), basting occasionally with the pan juices.

Makes 8 servings

Prep Time: 10 minutes
Bake Time: 1 hour 30 minutes

pasta
& rice

stovetop macaroni and cheese

1 tablespoon salt
12 ounces elbow macaroni, uncooked
1 (12-ounce) can evaporated milk
¼ cup **CREAM OF WHEAT®** Hot Cereal (Instant, 1-minute, 2½-minute or 10-minute cook time), uncooked

2 eggs
1 teaspoon Dijon mustard
½ teaspoon **TRAPPEY'S®** Red Devil™ Cayenne Pepper Sauce
½ teaspoon salt
8 ounces Cheddar cheese, shredded
½ cup milk

1. Bring large pot of water to a boil. Stir in 1 tablespoon salt. Add macaroni. Stir, then cook 8 minutes or until tender. Drain and return pasta to pot.

2. While pasta is cooking, whisk evaporated milk, Cream of Wheat, eggs, mustard, pepper sauce and ½ teaspoon salt in medium bowl.

3. Add mixture to cooked pasta. Cook and stir over medium-low heat until mixture thickens. Gradually stir in cheese, adding more as it melts. Add ½ cup milk; stir until creamy. Serve warm. *Makes 6 servings*

Tip: For a nice garnish and added extra crunch, combine ¼ cup fresh bread crumbs with ¼ cup Cream of Wheat. Melt 1 tablespoon butter in small saucepan over medium heat. Add Cream of Wheat mixture; cook and stir until mixture is golden brown. Sprinkle on top of each serving.

Prep Time: 5 minutes
Start to Finish Time: 20 minutes

easy risotto with bacon & peas

6 slices OSCAR MAYER®
Bacon, cut into 1-inch pieces

1 medium onion, chopped
(about 1 cup)

1½ cups medium grain rice,
uncooked

2 cloves garlic, minced

3 cans (15 ounces each)
chicken broth

4 ounces (½ of 8-ounce package)
PHILADELPHIA®
Cream Cheese, cubed

1 cup frozen peas, thawed

2 tablespoons chopped fresh
parsley

2 tablespoons KRAFT® Grated
Parmesan Cheese, divided

COOK bacon and onion in large skillet on medium-high heat 5 minutes or just until bacon is crisp, stirring occasionally.

ADD rice and garlic; cook 3 minutes or until rice is opaque, stirring frequently. Gradually add one half can broth; cook and stir 3 minutes or until broth is completely absorbed. Repeat with remaining broth, adding the cream cheese with the last addition of broth and cooking 5 minutes or until the cream cheese is completely melted and mixture is well blended.

STIR in peas; cook 2 minutes or until peas are heated through, stirring occasionally. Remove from heat. Stir in parsley and 1 tablespoon of the Parmesan cheese. Serve topped with the remaining 1 tablespoon Parmesan cheese.

Makes 6 servings (1 cup each)

Substitute: Prepare as directed, using fat-free reduced-sodium chicken broth.

Serving Suggestion: Serve with hot crusty bread and a mixed green salad topped with your favorite KRAFT® Dressing.

Prep Time: 10 minutes
Cook Time: 30 minutes
Total Time: 40 minutes

easy risotto with bacon & peas

creamy chicken florentine

1 can (10¾ ounces)
CAMPBELL'S® Condensed
Cream of Chicken Soup
(Regular or 98% Fat Free)

1½ cups water

½ of a 20-ounce bag frozen cut
leaf spinach, thawed and
well drained (about 3½ cups)

1 can (about 14½ ounces)
Italian-style diced tomatoes

4 skinless, boneless chicken
breast halves (about
1 pound), cut into
1-inch cubes

2½ cups uncooked penne pasta

½ cup shredded mozzarella
cheese

1. Heat the oven to 375°F. Stir the soup, water, spinach, tomatoes and chicken in a 3-quart shallow baking dish. Cover the baking dish.

2. Bake for 20 minutes. Cook the pasta according to the package directions and drain well in a colander. Uncover the baking dish and stir in the pasta.

3. Bake for 20 minutes or until the pasta mixture is hot and bubbling. Sprinkle with the cheese. Let stand for 5 minutes or until the cheese is melted.   *Makes 4 servings*

penne with arrabbiata sauce

½ pound uncooked penne or
other tube-shaped pasta

2 tablespoons olive oil or oil
from sun-dried tomatoes

8 whole cloves garlic

1 can (28 ounces) crushed
tomatoes in purée

3 tablespoons FRANK'S®
REDHOT® Original
Cayenne Pepper Sauce

8 kalamata or oil-cured olives,
pitted and chopped

6 fresh basil leaves or
1½ teaspoons dried
basil leaves

1 tablespoon capers

1. Cook pasta according to package directions; drain.

2. Heat oil in large nonstick skillet over medium heat. Add garlic; cook until golden, stirring frequently. Add remaining ingredients. Bring to a boil. Simmer, partially covered, 10 minutes. Stir occasionally.

3. Toss the pasta with half of the sauce mixture. Spoon into serving bowl. Pour remaining sauce mixture over pasta. Garnish with additional fresh basil or parsley, if desired.   *Makes 4 servings*

creamy chicken florentine

rice and cranberry pilaf

1 cup chicken broth
1 cup white cranberry juice
2 cups MINUTE® White Rice, uncooked

¼ cup dried cranberries
¼ cup almonds, sliced, toasted
1 teaspoon orange peel, grated (optional)

Pour broth and cranberry juice into medium saucepan. Bring to a boil over medium-high heat.

Stir in rice and cranberries; return to a boil. Cover; remove from heat. Let stand 5 minutes. Stir in almonds. Top with orange peel, if desired.   *Makes 6 servings*

Tip: To toast almonds quickly, spread them in a single layer in heavy-bottomed skillet. Cook over medium heat 1 to 2 minutes, stirring frequently, until nuts are lightly browned. Remove from skillet immediately. Cool before using.

spaghetti with zesty bolognese

1 small onion, chopped
¼ cup KRAFT® Light Zesty Italian Reduced Fat Dressing
1 pound extra-lean ground beef
1 can (15 ounces) tomato sauce

1 can (14 ounces) diced tomatoes, undrained
2 tablespoons PHILADELPHIA® Neufchâtel Cheese
12 ounces spaghetti, uncooked
¼ cup KRAFT® 100% Grated Parmesan Cheese

COOK onion in dressing in large skillet on medium heat. Increase heat to medium-high. Add meat; cook, stirring frequently, until browned. Stir in tomato sauce and tomatoes. Bring to boil. Reduce heat to medium-low; simmer 15 minutes. Remove from heat. Stir in Neufchâtel cheese until well blended.

MEANWHILE, cook pasta as directed on package.

SPOON sauce over pasta. Sprinkle with Parmesan cheese.   *Makes 6 servings*

rice and cranberry pilaf

bow tie pasta and sausage

1 package HILLSHIRE FARM®
  Smoked Sausage

½ cup boiling water

½ cup julienne-cut sun-dried
  tomatoes*

1 package (16 ounces) uncooked
  bow tie (farfalle) pasta

2 cups frozen baby lima beans

2 tablespoons olive oil

½ cup coarsely chopped onion

2 garlic cloves, minced

¼ teaspoon red pepper flakes
  (optional)

½ teaspoon salt

¼ teaspoon ground black pepper

2 tablespoons coarsely chopped
  Italian parsley

½ cup (2 ounces) shredded
  Asiago or Parmesan cheese

*Dry-pack julienne-cut sun-dried tomatoes
work well in this recipe and can be found in
the produce section of most grocery stores.

1. Cut sausage in ½-inch cubes; set aside. Pour boiling water over tomatoes; let stand
20 minutes. Cook pasta in a large pan of boiling water for 2 minutes; add lima beans
and cook 8 minutes longer or until pasta is tender. Drain and keep warm.

2. While pasta is cooking, heat olive oil in a large nonstick skillet over medium-high
heat until hot; add sausage and onion. Cook, stirring frequently, for 4 minutes or until
sausage is lightly browned and onion is tender. Add garlic and red pepper flakes, if
desired; cook, stirring constantly, for 1 minute. Stir in tomatoes and soaking liquid,
salt and pepper; heat through.

3. Toss pasta and lima beans with sausage mixture and parsley. Top with shredded
cheese.   *Makes 8 servings (about 1½ cups each)*

seasoned chicken & wild rice

1 package (4.2 ounces)
  RICE-A-RONI®
  Long Grain & Wild Rice

1¼ cups water

1 tablespoon margarine or butter

1 pound boneless, skinless
  chicken breasts, cut into
  bite-sized pieces

½ cup chopped celery

½ cup chopped onion

½ cup chopped carrot (optional)

1. In a large skillet, combine rice-vermicelli mix, seasoning mix, water, margarine and
chicken. Bring to a boil.

2. Cover, reduce heat to low and simmer 25 to 30 minutes or until rice is tender and
water is absorbed. Add celery, onion and carrot, if desired, during last 5 minutes of
simmering. Let stand 5 minutes before serving.   *Makes 4 servings*

bow tie pasta and sausage

amazin' crab rice cakes

1 cup chicken broth

1 cup **MINUTE®** White Rice, uncooked

2 eggs

2 cans (6 ounces each) crabmeat, drained, flaked*

2 tablespoons seafood seasoning

¼ cup (½ stick) butter or margarine

Fresh lemon wedges (optional)

Or substitute 12 ounces canned salmon.

Bring broth to a boil in small saucepan. Stir in rice; cover. Remove from heat; let stand 5 minutes. Fluff with fork.

Beat eggs lightly in medium bowl. Add rice, crabmeat and seasoning; mix well. Refrigerate 5 minutes. Shape into 8 patties.

Melt butter in large skillet over medium heat. Add patties; cook 5 minutes on each side or until golden brown and heated through. Serve with lemon, if desired.

Makes 4 servings

Tip: To serve as appetizers, make the patties in bite-size portions.

lasagna florentine

9 long lasagna noodles

1 package JENNIE-O TURKEY STORE® Extra Lean Ground Turkey Breast

2 teaspoons bottled or fresh minced garlic

1 jar (28 ounces) spaghetti sauce

1 container (15 ounces) ricotta cheese

1 package (10 ounces) frozen chopped spinach, thawed, well drained

1 egg

¼ to ½ teaspoon crushed red pepper flakes, as desired

¼ teaspoon nutmeg

2 cups (8 ounces) shredded mozzarella or Italian blend cheese

Preheat oven to 350°F. Cook noodles according to package directions. Meanwhile, in large skillet, cook turkey and garlic over medium heat until turkey is no longer pink. Add spaghetti sauce; simmer 10 minutes, stirring occasionally. In small bowl, combine ricotta cheese, spinach, egg, pepper flakes and nutmeg; mix well. Spread ½ cup spaghetti sauce mixture in bottom of 13×9-inch baking dish. Layer half of noodles over sauce; spoon half of cheese mixture over noodles. Spoon 1 cup sauce over cheese mixture; repeat layering with remaining noodles, cheese mixture and sauce. Cover with foil; bake 50 minutes or until bubbly. Sprinkle mozzarella cheese over lasagna; return to oven and continue baking 5 minutes or until cheese is melted.

Makes 8 servings

amazin' crab rice cakes

skillet pasta roma

½ pound Italian sausage, sliced or crumbled

1 large onion, coarsely chopped

1 large clove garlic, minced

2 cans (14½ ounces each) DEL MONTE® Diced Tomatoes with Basil, Garlic & Oregano

1 can (8 ounces) DEL MONTE® Tomato Sauce

1 cup water

8 ounces uncooked rotini or other spiral pasta

8 mushrooms, sliced (optional)

Grated Parmesan cheese and fresh parsley sprigs (optional)

1. Brown sausage in large skillet. Add onion and garlic. Cook until onion is soft; drain. Stir in undrained tomatoes, tomato sauce, water and pasta.

2. Cover and bring to a boil; reduce heat. Simmer, covered, 25 to 30 minutes or until pasta is tender, stirring occasionally.

3. Stir in mushrooms, if desired; simmer 5 minutes. Serve in skillet garnished with cheese and parsley, if desired. *Makes 4 servings*

paella

1 tablespoon olive oil

½ pound chicken breast cubes

1 cup uncooked rice*

1 medium onion, chopped

1 clove garlic, minced

1½ cups chicken broth

1 can (8 ounces) stewed tomatoes, chopped, reserving liquid

½ teaspoon paprika

⅛ to ¼ teaspoon ground red pepper

⅛ teaspoon ground saffron

½ pound medium shrimp, peeled and deveined

1 small red pepper, cut into strips

1 small green pepper, cut into strips

½ cup frozen green peas

If using medium grain rice, use 1¼ cups of broth; if using parboiled rice, use 1¾ cups of broth.

Heat oil in Dutch oven over medium-high heat until hot. Add chicken and stir until browned. Add rice, onion and garlic. Cook, stirring, until onion is tender and rice is lightly browned. Add broth, tomatoes, tomato liquid, paprika, ground red pepper and saffron. Bring to a boil; stir. Reduce heat; cover and simmer 10 minutes. Add shrimp, pepper strips and peas. Cover and simmer 10 minutes or until rice is tender and liquid is absorbed. *Makes 6 servings*

Favorite recipe from **USA Rice**

patrick's nutty chicken fried rice

1 pound boneless, skinless chicken breasts, cut into strips

1 tablespoon vegetable oil

1¾ cups water

2 tablespoons SKIPPY® Creamy or SUPER CHUNK® Peanut Butter

1 tablespoon rice wine vinegar or white vinegar

1 tablespoon soy sauce

¼ teaspoon ground ginger (optional)

1 package KNORR® RICE SIDES™–Chicken

½ cup thawed frozen or drained canned green peas

1. Season chicken, if desired, with salt and ground black pepper. Heat oil in 12-inch nonstick skillet over medium-high heat and cook chicken, stirring occasionally, 5 minutes or until chicken is thoroughly cooked. Remove chicken and set aside.

2. Stir water, Skippy® Creamy Peanut Butter, vinegar, soy sauce and ginger into same skillet. Bring to a boil over high heat. Stir in Knorr® Rice Sides™–Chicken. Cover and cook over medium heat, stirring occasionally, 8 minutes or until rice is tender.

3. Stir in chicken and peas; heat through. Garnish, if desired, with chopped green onions and chopped peanuts.

Makes 4 servings

Prep Time: 10 minutes
Cook Time: 15 minutes

no-boiling stuffed manicotti

1 pound ground beef

2 jars (1 pound 10 ounces each) RAGÚ® Old World Style® Pasta Sauce

1 container (15 ounces) ricotta cheese

1 box (8 ounces) uncooked manicotti

1. Preheat oven to 375°F. In 12-inch nonstick skillet, brown ground beef; drain. Stir in 1 cup Pasta Sauce and 1 cup ricotta; set aside.

2. In 13×9-inch baking dish, spread 2 cups Pasta Sauce. Fill uncooked manicotti with beef mixture and arrange in baking dish. Top with any remaining beef mixture, then top with remaining sauce.

3. Cover tightly with aluminum foil and bake 1 hour. Remove foil and top with spoonfuls of remaining ricotta cheese. Bake uncovered an additional 10 minutes. Let stand 10 minutes before serving.

Makes 6 servings

Prep Time: 10 minutes
Cook Time: 1 hour, 15 minutes

patrick's nutty chicken fried rice

velveeta® tuna noodle casserole

4 cups egg noodles, cooked, drained

1 package (16 ounces) frozen peas and carrots

2 cans (6 ounces each) tuna, drained, flaked

1 can (10¾ ounces) condensed cream of mushroom soup

⅓ cup milk

¾ pound (12 ounces) VELVEETA® Pasteurized Prepared Cheese Product, cut into ½-inch cubes

1 can (2.8 ounces) French fried onion rings

HEAT oven to 400°F. Combine all ingredients except onions in 13×9-inch baking dish; cover with foil.

BAKE 45 minutes or until heated through; stir.

TOP with onions.

Makes 8 servings (about 1 cup each)

Variation: Prepare using reduced-fat condensed cream of mushroom soup and VELVEETA® 2% Milk Pasteurized Prepared Cheese Product.

thai chicken fettucine

2 cups picante sauce

½ cup crunchy peanut butter

4 tablespoons honey

4 tablespoons orange juice

2 teaspoons soy sauce

1 teaspoon ground ginger

4 whole boneless, skinless chicken breasts, pounded

14 ounces cooked fettucine

½ cup cilantro, chopped

½ cup peanuts

½ cup green pepper strips

Combine picante sauce, peanut butter, honey, orange juice, soy sauce and ginger in saucepan. Cook over medium heat, stirring until blended. Store in refrigerator until ready to use.

Put half the sauce in large nonreactive pan and marinate chicken breasts for at least 8 hours, turning occasionally. Grill chicken breasts for 10 minutes on each side or until done. Warm the remainder of the sauce and add to the cooked fettucine. To serve, put fettucine mixture on a platter, cut the chicken breasts into strips and lay on top. Sprinkle with cilantro, peanuts and pepper strips. *Makes 4 servings*

Favorite recipe from **Peanut Advisory Board**

velveeta® tuna noodle casserole

quick jambalaya

1 package **HILLSHIRE FARM®** Smoked Sausage

1 tablespoon butter or margarine

1 medium onion, chopped

1 red bell pepper, seeded, chopped

1 green bell pepper, seeded, chopped

2 cloves garlic, minced

1 can (28 ounces) crushed tomatoes

½ teaspoon hot pepper sauce

½ teaspoon ground black pepper

¼ teaspoon crushed red pepper flakes

Salt to taste

½ pound large raw shrimp, peeled, deveined

6 cups hot cooked long grain white rice

1. Cut sausage in ½-inch slices. Melt butter in 5-quart pan over medium-high heat. Add sausage, onion, red bell pepper, green bell pepper and garlic; cook, stirring occasionally, 5 minutes or until vegetables are soft and sausage is lightly browned.

2. Stir in tomatoes, pepper sauce, black pepper, crushed red pepper flakes and salt to taste. Bring to a boil; add shrimp and cook 3 minutes or until shrimp turn pink.

3. Gently stir in hot rice and cook 3 to 5 minutes or until heated through.

Makes 6 servings (about 1¾ cups each)

pasta with gorgonzola sauce

1½ cups whipping cream

1½ cups **BELGIOIOSO®** CreamyGorg®

1 pound fettuccine, cooked and drained

Fresh grated **BELGIOIOSO®** Parmesan

Fresh cracked black pepper

Chopped fresh basil

In a medium saucepan, bring cream to a boil over medium heat. Simmer for about 5 minutes. Reduce heat to low and stir in Belgioioso CreamyGorg until melted.

Place cooked pasta into large, warm bowl. Pour sauce over and toss. Sprinkle with Belgioioso Parmesan, pepper and basil.

Makes 6 servings

chicken and linguine in creamy tomato sauce

1 tablespoon olive oil

1 pound boneless, skinless chicken breasts, cut into ½-inch strips

1 jar (1 pound 10 ounces) RAGÚ® Old World Style® Pasta Sauce

2 cups water

8 ounces uncooked linguine or spaghetti

½ cup whipping or heavy cream

1 tablespoon chopped fresh basil leaves *or* ½ teaspoon dried basil leaves, crushed

1. In 12-inch skillet, heat olive oil over medium heat and brown chicken. Remove chicken and set aside.

2. In same skillet, stir in Pasta Sauce and water. Bring to a boil over high heat. Stir in uncooked linguine and return to a boil. Reduce heat to low and simmer covered, stirring occasionally, 15 minutes or until linguine is tender.

3. Stir in cream and basil. Return chicken to skillet and cook 5 minutes or until chicken is thoroughly cooked.   *Makes 4 servings*

Prep Time: 10 minutes
Cook Time: 30 minutes

taco rice and beans

2 tablespoons olive oil

1 medium onion, diced

1 cup water

1 packet (1.25 ounces) ORTEGA® Taco Seasoning Mix

1 can (15 ounces) ORTEGA® Black Beans, drained

2 cups cooked rice

¼ cup ORTEGA® Thick & Chunky Salsa

Heat oil in skillet over medium heat until hot. Add onion. Cook and stir 3 minutes. Add water and seasoning mix. Cook and stir until combined and slightly thickened. Stir in beans, rice and salsa. Cook 5 minutes longer or until heated through.

Makes 4 servings

Tip: For a great vegetarian meal, fold Taco Rice and Beans into an Ortega® soft flour tortilla.

Prep Time: 5 minutes
Start to Finish Time: 15 minutes

chicken and linguine in creamy tomato sauce

louisiana gumbo

2 cups MINUTE® White Rice, uncooked

2 tablespoons butter

2 tablespoons all-purpose flour

½ cup onion, chopped

½ cup celery, chopped

½ cup green bell pepper, chopped

1 clove garlic, minced

1 package (14 ounces) smoked turkey sausage, sliced

1 can (14½ ounces) diced tomatoes

1 can (14½ ounces) chicken broth

1 package (10 ounces) frozen sliced okra, thawed*

1 tablespoon Cajun seasoning

¼ teaspoon dried thyme

½ pound shrimp, peeled, deveined

Salt and black pepper, to taste

*Or substitute 1 package (10 ounces) frozen cut green beans.

Prepare rice according to package directions.

Melt butter in large skillet over medium-high heat. Stir in flour; cook and stir until light golden brown, about 5 minutes. Add onion, celery, bell pepper and garlic; cook 2 to 3 minutes or until tender.

Stir in sausage, tomatoes, broth, okra, seasoning and thyme; cover. Simmer 5 minutes, stirring occasionally.

Add shrimp; cook 5 minutes or until shrimp are pink. Season with salt and pepper to taste. Serve with rice. *Makes 6 servings*

ham asparagus gratin

1 can (10¾ ounces) CAMPBELL'S® Condensed Cream of Asparagus Soup

½ cup milk

¼ teaspoon onion powder

¼ teaspoon ground black pepper

1½ cups cooked cut asparagus

1½ cups cubed cooked ham

2¼ cups corkscrew-shaped pasta (rotini), cooked and drained

1 cup shredded Cheddar cheese or Swiss cheese

1. Stir the soup, milk, onion powder, black pepper, asparagus, ham, pasta and ½ **cup** cheese in a 2-quart shallow baking dish.

2. Bake at 400°F. for 25 minutes or until the ham mixture is hot and bubbling. Stir the ham mixture. Sprinkle with the remaining cheese.

3. Bake for 5 minutes or until the cheese is melted. *Makes 4 servings*

louisiana gumbo

spinach ricotta gnocchi

1 package (16 ounces) frozen dumpling-shaped pasta (gnocchi)

2 cups frozen cut leaf spinach, thawed and well drained

1½ cups PREGO® Heart Smart Onion and Garlic Italian Sauce or Heart Smart Traditional Italian Sauce

¼ cup grated Romano cheese

½ cup ricotta cheese

1 cup shredded mozzarella cheese (about 4 ounces)

1. Prepare the gnocchi according to the package directions in a 6-quart saucepot. Add the spinach during the last 3 minutes of cooking time. Drain the gnocchi mixture well in a colander. Return the gnocchi mixture to the saucepot.

2. Stir the Italian sauce, Romano cheese and ricotta cheese in the saucepot. Cook over medium heat until the mixture is hot and bubbling, stirring occasionally. Top with the mozzarella cheese. *Makes 6 servings*

Prep Time: 5 minutes
Cook Time: 25 minutes
Total Time: 30 minutes

parmesan and veg·all® rice pilaf

1 tablespoon olive oil

⅔ cup chopped onion

1 cup uncooked long grain rice

3 cups chicken broth or water

½ teaspoon oregano

¼ teaspoon basil

¼ teaspoon black pepper

1 can (15 ounces) VEG·ALL® Original Mixed Vegetables, drained

1 can (4 ounces) artichoke hearts, drained and chopped

½ cup grated Parmesan cheese

Heat oil in large skillet. Add onion; cook 1 minute. Add rice; stir 1 minute. Stir in chicken broth and spices. Heat to a boil.

Cover, reduce heat and simmer 15 minutes. Stir in Veg·All, artichokes and cheese.

Cover; heat 5 minutes or until liquid is absorbed. *Makes 6 servings*

spinach ricotta gnocchi

hoppin' john

1 package (14 ounces) smoked turkey sausage, thinly sliced

3 cans (15½ ounces each) black-eyed peas, drained, rinsed

2 cans (14½ ounces each) chicken broth

2 cups onions, chopped

1 teaspoon crushed red pepper

½ teaspoon ground red pepper

2½ cups MINUTE® White Rice, uncooked

Fresh parsley, chopped (optional)

Brown sausage in medium saucepan over medium-high heat. Add peas, broth, onions and seasonings; bring to a boil. Stir in rice; cover. Simmer 10 minutes or until rice is tender. Garnish with parsley, if desired.

Makes 8 servings

easy pumpkin-pasta bake

Nonstick cooking spray

1 pound (about 4 links) sweet or spicy lean Italian turkey sausage, casings removed

1 tablespoon finely chopped garlic

1 jar (24 to 26 ounces) marinara sauce

½ cup water or dry red or white wine

1 can (15 ounces) LIBBY'S® 100% Pure Pumpkin

4 tablespoons (¾ ounce) shredded Parmesan cheese, *divided*

1 box (14½ ounces) whole wheat penne or other short-cut pasta, prepared according to package directions

1 cup (4 ounces) shredded low-moisture part-skim mozzarella cheese

PREHEAT oven to 375°F. Spray 3-quart casserole dish or 13×9-inch baking dish with nonstick cooking spray.

COOK sausage in large skillet over medium-high heat until cooked through. Stir in garlic; cook for 1 minute. Stir in marinara sauce (reserve jar). Add water or wine to jar; cover and shake. Pour into skillet along with pumpkin and *2 tablespoons* Parmesan cheese. Stir well. Stir in prepared pasta. Spoon into prepared dish. Sprinkle with *remaining 2 tablespoons* Parmesan cheese and mozzarella cheese; cover.

BAKE for 15 minutes. Carefully remove cover; bake for an additional 5 minutes or until cheese is melted and bubbly.

Makes 10 servings

hoppin' john

side dishes

savory spinach with blue cheese and walnuts

1 tablespoon butter

1 large sweet onion, halved and thinly sliced (about 1 cup)

2 cloves garlic, sliced

2 large tomatoes, seeded and chopped (about 3 cups)

¾ cup SWANSON® Chicken Broth (Regular, Natural Goodness® or Certified Organic)

1 bag (11 ounces) fresh baby spinach

Ground black pepper

¼ cup crumbled blue cheese (about 2 ounces)

2 tablespoons chopped walnuts

1. Heat the butter in a 12-inch nonstick skillet. Add the onion and garlic and cook until they're tender, stirring occasionally.

2. Add the tomatoes, broth and spinach. Cook for 2 minutes or until the spinach is wilted. Season with the black pepper. Sprinkle with the cheese and walnuts.

Makes 6 servings

Prep Time: 15 minutes
Cook Time: 15 minutes
Total Time: 30 minutes

spicy steak fries

2 large potatoes	2 tablespoons olive oil
2 tablespoons MRS. DASH® Extra Spicy Seasoning Blend	1 clove garlic, minced

1. Wash and cut potatoes into wedges; do not peel. Dry potato slices on paper towels.

2. In a large bowl, toss potatoes with MRS. DASH® Extra Spicy Seasoning Blend, olive oil and garlic.

3. Spray baking sheet with nonstick cooking spray and lay wedges on baking sheet. Place potatoes in preheated 425°F oven and bake for 20 minutes. Turn the potatoes and bake another 15 minutes or until potatoes are browned and tender.

Makes 4 servings

Prep Time: 10 minutes
Cook Time: 35 to 40 minutes

glazed acorn squash

2 medium acorn squash, halved and seeded	1 tablespoon margarine or butter, melted
1½ cups water	½ teaspoon ground cinnamon
⅓ cup KARO® Light or Dark Corn Syrup	¼ teaspoon salt

1. Place squash cut-side down in 13×9×2-inch baking dish; add water. Bake in 400°F oven 30 minutes or until squash is nearly fork-tender.

2. Turn squash cut-side up. In small bowl combine corn syrup, margarine, cinnamon and salt. Spoon corn syrup mixture into squash cavities.

3. Bake in 350°F oven 15 minutes or until fork-tender, basting occasionally.

Makes 4 servings

Prep Time: 5 minutes
Bake Time: 45 minutes

spicy steak fries

easy summer vegetable medley

2 medium red or green bell peppers, cut into chunks

2 medium zucchini or summer squash, sliced lengthwise in half and then into thick slices

1 (12-ounce) package mushrooms, cleaned and cut into quarters

3 carrots, thinly sliced

1⅓ cups **FRENCH'S®** French Fried Onions or **FRENCH'S®** Cheddar French Fried Onions

¼ cup fresh basil, minced

2 tablespoons olive oil

Salt and black pepper to taste

2 ice cubes

1 large foil oven roasting bag

1. Toss all ingredients except foil bag in large bowl. Open bag; spoon mixture into bag in even layer. Seal bag with tight double folds. Place bag on baking sheet.

2. Place bag on grill over medium-high heat. Cover grill and cook 15 minutes until vegetables are tender, turning bag over once.

3. Return bag to baking sheet and carefully cut top of bag open. Sprinkle with additional French Fried Onions, if desired.   *Makes 4 to 6 servings*

Prep Time: 10 minutes
Cook Time: 15 minutes

peas florentine style

2 (10-ounce) packages frozen peas

¼ cup **FILIPPO BERIO®** Olive Oil

4 ounces Canadian bacon, cubed

1 garlic clove, minced

1 tablespoon chopped fresh Italian parsley

1 teaspoon sugar

Salt

Place peas in large colander or strainer; run under hot water until slightly thawed. Drain well. In medium skillet, heat olive oil over medium heat until hot. Add bacon and garlic; cook and stir 2 to 3 minutes or until garlic turns golden. Add peas and parsley; cook and stir over high heat 5 to 7 minutes or until heated through. Drain well. Stir in sugar; season to taste with salt.   *Makes 5 servings*

easy summer vegetable medley

quick greens and beans

3 slices bacon, diced

5 collard leaves, stems removed, chopped

½ cup ORTEGA® Black Beans, rinsed, drained

2 tablespoons ORTEGA® Fire-Roasted Diced Green Chiles

2 tablespoons ORTEGA® Taco Sauce

Salt and black pepper, to taste

Cook bacon in medium skillet over medium-high heat until crispy. Bring small saucepan of salted water to a boil. Stir in collard leaves. Boil 5 minutes. Drain; add to bacon in skillet. Stir in black beans, chiles and taco sauce. Add salt and pepper to taste; toss to combine well.

Makes 4 servings

Note: You can replace the black beans with pinto or kidney beans, or add corn for extra color.

Prep Time: 5 minutes
Start to Finish Time: 15 minutes

candied sweet potatoes

MAZOLA PURE® Cooking Spray

1 can (29 ounces) cut sweet potatoes, drained

3 tablespoons butter or margarine

½ cup KARO® Light or Dark Corn Syrup

3 tablespoons sugar

¾ teaspoon salt

¾ teaspoon ground cinnamon

1. Coat shallow 1½- to 2-quart baking dish with cooking spray. Place sweet potatoes in prepared dish.

2. In small saucepan over low heat melt butter. Stir in corn syrup, sugar, salt and cinnamon. Cook and stir 1 to 2 minutes or until smooth. Pour evenly over sweet potatoes; stir gently to coat.

3. Bake in 350°F oven 20 minutes or until hot and bubbly.

Makes 4 to 6 servings

Prep Time: 10 minutes
Cook Time: 20 minutes

quick greens and beans

savory vegetable stuffing bake

¼ pound bulk pork sausage

1 large onion, chopped (about 1 cup)

½ teaspoon dried thyme leaves, crushed

1 can (10¾ ounces) CAMPBELL'S® Condensed Cream of Celery Soup (Regular or 98% Fat Free)

1 can (about 8 ounces) stewed tomatoes

2 cups frozen vegetable combination (broccoli, corn, red pepper)

3 cups PEPPERIDGE FARM® Herb Seasoned Stuffing

1. Cook the sausage, onion and thyme in a 12-inch skillet over medium-high heat until the sausage is browned, stirring frequently to break up the meat. Pour off any fat.

2. Stir the soup, tomatoes and vegetables in the skillet. Heat to a boil. Remove the skillet from the heat. Add the stuffing and stir lightly to coat. Spoon into a 1½-quart casserole.

3. Bake at 350°F. for 30 minutes or until it's hot and bubbling.   *Makes 6 servings*

Prep Time: 20 minutes
Cook Time: 30 minutes
Total Time: 50 minutes

sweet-sour red cabbage

1 tablespoon butter or margarine

½ cup wine vinegar

¼ cup honey

1 teaspoon salt

1 medium head red cabbage, shredded (8 cups)

2 apples, cored and diced

Melt butter in large nonstick skillet or stainless steel saucepan over medium heat. Stir in vinegar, honey and salt. Add cabbage and apples; toss well. Reduce heat to low; cover and simmer 45 to 50 minutes.   *Makes 4 to 6 servings*

Microwave Directions: Place shredded cabbage in 3-quart microwave-safe baking dish. Add apples, butter and vinegar. Cover and cook on HIGH (100%) 15 minutes. Stir in honey and salt. Cover and cook on HIGH 10 minutes.

Favorite recipe from **National Honey Board**

savory vegetable stuffing bake

honey-balsamic roasted vegetables

1½ pounds assorted cut-up
fresh vegetables*

¼ cup I CAN'T BELIEVE
IT'S NOT BUTTER®
Mediterranean Blend
spread, melted

1 tablespoon balsamic vinegar

1 teaspoon honey

½ teaspoon dried thyme leaves,
crushed

Salt and ground black pepper
to taste

*Use any combination of the following:
zucchini, red, green or yellow bell peppers,
Spanish or red onions, white or portobello
mushrooms and carrots.*

1. Preheat oven to 425°F. In broiler pan, without the rack, combine all ingredients.
Roast 25 minutes or until vegetables are tender, stirring once.   *Makes 6 servings*

Prep Time: 5 minutes
Cook Time: 25 minutes

sweet potato fries with bbq mayonnaise

2 pounds sweet potatoes or yams,
peeled and cut into
2-inch-long thin wedges

1 cup HELLMANN'S® or
BEST FOODS® Real
Mayonnaise, divided

¼ cup barbecue sauce

1. Preheat oven to 425°F. Line 2 jelly-roll pans with aluminum foil, then spray with
nonstick cooking spray; set aside.

2. Combine potatoes with ½ cup Hellmann's® or Best Foods® Real Mayonnaise in large
bowl; toss to coat. Arrange potatoes on prepared pans.

3. Bake 20 minutes. Rotate pans and bake an additional 15 minutes or until potatoes
are golden and crisp.

4. Meanwhile, combine remaining ½ cup Mayonnaise with barbecue sauce in small
bowl. Serve with fries.   *Makes 8 servings*

Prep Time: 15 minutes
Cook Time: 35 minutes

honey-balsamic roasted vegetables

chive & onion mashed potatoes

2 pounds potatoes, peeled, quartered (about 6 cups)
½ cup milk

1 tub (8 ounces) PHILADELPHIA® Chive & Onion Cream Cheese Spread
¼ cup KRAFT® Ranch Dressing

PLACE potatoes and enough water to cover in 3-quart saucepan. Bring to a boil.

REDUCE heat to medium; cook 20 to 25 minutes or until tender. Drain.

MASH potatoes, gradually stirring in milk, cream cheese spread and dressing until light and fluffy. Serve immediately. *Makes 10 servings (½ cup each)*

Make Ahead: Mix ingredients as directed; spoon into 1½-quart casserole dish. Cover. Refrigerate several hours or overnight. When ready to serve, bake, uncovered, at 350°F 1 hour or until heated through.

Substitute: Substitute KRAFT® Three Cheese Ranch Dressing for Ranch Dressing.

Prep Time: 10 minutes
Cook Time: 25 minutes

baked maple and cinnamon squash

2 tablespoons IMPERIAL® Spread, melted
2 tablespoons maple syrup
2 tablespoons firmly packed brown sugar

½ teaspoon ground cinnamon
1 medium butternut squash, halved and seeded

1. Preheat oven to 400°F. Lightly grease baking sheet.

2. In small bowl, combine Imperial® Spread, syrup, brown sugar and cinnamon. On baking sheet, arrange squash cut side up; brush with ½ of Spread mixture.

3. Bake 45 minutes or until tender, brushing with remaining Spread mixture halfway through cooking. Season with salt, if desired. *Makes 4 servings*

Prep Time: 10 minutes
Cook Time: 45 minutes

chive & onion mashed potatoes

mozzarella zucchini skillet

2 tablespoons vegetable oil

5 medium zucchini, sliced (about 7½ cups)

1 medium onion, chopped (about ½ cup)

¼ teaspoon garlic powder or 2 cloves garlic, minced

1½ cups PREGO® Traditional Italian Sauce or Organic Tomato & Basil Italian Sauce

½ cup shredded mozzarella cheese or Cheddar cheese

1. Heat the oil in a 12-inch skillet over medium-high heat. Add the zucchini, onion and garlic powder and cook until the vegetables are tender-crisp.

2. Stir the Italian sauce into the skillet and heat through.

3. Sprinkle with the cheese. Cover and cook until the cheese melts.

Makes 7 servings

Prep Time: 10 minutes
Cook Time: 15 minutes
Total Time: 25 minutes

double onion crunchy rings

2 cups FRENCH'S® French Fried Onions

¼ cup plus 2 tablespoons all-purpose flour, divided

2 cups medium onions, cut into ½-inch rings

2 egg whites, beaten

1. Heat oven to 400°F. Place French Fried Onions and *2 tablespoons* flour in plastic bag. Lightly crush with hands or with rolling pin. Place ¼ *cup* flour in separate plastic bag. Toss onion rings in ¼ cup flour; shake off excess.

2. Dip floured onion rings into beaten egg whites. Coat in crushed onions, pressing firmly to adhere.

3. Place rings on lightly greased baking rack set over rimmed baking sheet. Bake 10 minutes or until onions are tender.

Makes about 2½ dozen pieces

Prep Time: 15 minutes
Cook Time: 10 minutes

mozzarella zucchini skillet

salsa-buttered corn on the cob

6 ears fresh corn, shucked

4 tablespoons butter, softened

¼ cup ORTEGA® Salsa,
  any variety

2 tablespoons ORTEGA®
  Taco Seasoning Mix,
  or to taste

Bring large pot of water to a boil. Add corn; cook 5 to 10 minutes.

Combine butter and salsa in small bowl; mix well. Place seasoning mix in another small bowl. Spread salsa butter onto cooked corn and sprinkle on seasoning mix to taste.

Makes 6 servings

Tip: For a different side dish, cut the corn off the cob and heat in a skillet with the salsa butter and taco seasoning mix.

Prep Time: 5 minutes
Start to Finish Time: 20 minutes

citrus-glazed asparagus

½ cup HELLMANN'S® or
  BEST FOODS®
  Light Mayonnaise

2 tablespoons milk

1 tablespoon lemon juice

½ teaspoon grated lemon peel
  (optional)

½ teaspoon fresh thyme leaves
  or ⅛ teaspoon dried thyme,
  crushed (optional)

⅛ teaspoon coarsely ground black
  pepper

1 pound asparagus, trimmed and
  cooked (grilled, roasted or
  steamed)

1. Combine all ingredients except asparagus in small microwave-safe bowl. Microwave at HIGH 30 seconds or until heated through. Stir, then drizzle sauce over hot asparagus.

Makes 4 servings

Serving Suggestion: Serve hot sauce over your favorite cooked vegetables or cooked chicken, fish or pork.

salsa-buttered corn on the cob

creamy golden mushroom mashed potatoes

6 medium baking potatoes,
cut into 1-inch pieces
(about 6 cups)

1 small onion, cut into wedges

Water

1 can (10¾ ounces)
CAMPBELL'S® Condensed
Golden Mushroom Soup

¾ cup milk

¼ cup heavy cream

4 tablespoons butter

1. Put the potatoes and onion in a 4-quart saucepot with enough water to cover them. Heat the potatoes over medium-high heat to a boil. Reduce the heat to low. Cover and cook the potatoes for 20 minutes or until they're fork-tender. Drain the potatoes and onion well in a colander.

2. Put the potatoes and onion in a 3-quart bowl and beat with an electric mixer at medium speed until almost smooth.

3. Put the soup, milk, cream and butter in a 4-cup microwavable measuring cup. Microwave on HIGH for 2½ minutes or until hot. Slowly pour the hot soup mixture into the potatoes, beating with an electric mixer at medium speed until the potatoes are smooth. Season to taste. *Makes 6 servings*

Prep Time: 20 minutes
Cook Time: 30 minutes
Total Time: 50 minutes

honey and vanilla glazed carrots

¼ cup (½ stick) butter or
margarine

¼ cup honey

1½ pounds baby carrots
(about 5 cups), cooked
until crisp-tender

1½ teaspoons WATKINS®
Vanilla Extract

Pinch WATKINS® Ginger

Salt and WATKINS®
Black Pepper to taste

Melt butter in medium saucepan. Add honey and stir until blended. Add carrots, vanilla and ginger. Cook over low heat, stirring occasionally, until carrots are well glazed. Season with salt and pepper. *Makes 10 servings (5 cups)*

creamy golden mushroom
mashed potatoes

green beans with toasted pecans

3 tablespoons I CAN'T
BELIEVE IT'S NOT
BUTTER!® Spread, melted
1 teaspoon sugar
¼ teaspoon LAWRY'S®
Garlic Powder with Parsley

Pinch ground red pepper
Salt to taste
⅓ cup chopped pecans
1 pound green beans

In small bowl, blend I Can't Believe It's Not Butter!® Spread, sugar, garlic powder, pepper and salt.

In 12-inch nonstick skillet, heat 2 teaspoons garlic mixture over medium-high heat and cook pecans, stirring frequently, 2 minutes or until pecans are golden. Remove pecans and set aside.

In same skillet, heat remaining garlic mixture and stir in green beans. Cook, covered, over medium heat, stirring occasionally, 6 minutes or until green beans are tender. Stir in pecans.   *Makes 4 servings*

scalloped potatoes with gorgonzola

1½ cups whipping cream
1 can (14½ ounces) chicken broth
4 teaspoons minced garlic
1½ teaspoons sage

1 cup BELGIOIOSO®
Gorgonzola
2¼ pounds russet potatoes, peeled,
halved, thinly sliced

Preheat oven to 375°F. Simmer whipping cream, chicken broth, garlic and sage in heavy medium saucepan 5 minutes until slightly thickened. Add Belgioioso Gorgonzola and stir until melted. Remove from heat.

In large bowl, add potatoes and season with salt and pepper. Arrange half of potatoes in 13×9×2-inch glass baking dish. Pour half of cream mixture over potatoes. Repeat layering with remaining potatoes and cream mixture. Bake until potatoes are tender, about 1¼ hours. Let stand 15 minutes before serving.   *Makes 8 servings*

green beans with toasted pecans

jalapeño refried beans

4 slices bacon
¼ cup chopped onion
2 tablespoons POLANER®
Minced Garlic
½ teaspoon ground cumin
1 can (16 ounces) ORTEGA®
Refried Beans

1 jar (12 ounces) ORTEGA®
Sliced Jalapeño Peppers,
diced
1 cup (4 ounces) shredded
Monterey Jack cheese
or queso blanco

Fry bacon in medium skillet over medium heat until crisp. Drain on paper towels.

Add onion, garlic and cumin to bacon drippings. Cook and stir until onion becomes translucent, about 3 minutes.

Crumble bacon; add to onion mixture. Stir in refried beans and jalapeños. Heat thoroughly. Top with shredded cheese to serve. *Makes 4 servings*

Prep Time: 10 minutes
Start to Finish Time: 15 minutes

crunchy praline-topped sweet potatoes

1 package SIMPLY
POTATOES® Sweet
Mashed Potatoes
½ teaspoon salt
1 cup corn flakes cereal,
coarsely crushed

½ cup chopped pecans
⅓ cup brown sugar
¼ cup butter or margarine,
melted
2 tablespoons all-purpose flour

1. Heat oven to 350°F. Spray 1½-quart casserole dish with nonstick cooking spray. Combine Simply Potatoes® and salt in casserole; mix well.

2. In medium bowl, combine all remaining ingredients; stir to mix well. Spread topping evenly over Simply Potatoes®.

3. Bake, uncovered, 25 to 30 minutes or until topping is light golden brown and potatoes are heated through. *Makes 4 to 5 servings*

Tip: A quick and easy way to crush cereal is to place it in a 1-quart resealable plastic bag. With fingers, gently crush cereal into course crumbs.

jalapeño refried beans

cookies & bars

oatmeal scotchies

1¼ cups all-purpose flour
1 teaspoon baking soda
½ teaspoon salt
½ teaspoon ground cinnamon
1 cup (2 sticks) butter or margarine, softened
¾ cup granulated sugar
¾ cup packed brown sugar

2 large eggs
1 teaspoon vanilla extract *or* grated peel of 1 orange
3 cups quick or old-fashioned oats
1⅔ cups (11-ounce package) NESTLÉ® TOLL HOUSE® Butterscotch Flavored Morsels

PREHEAT oven to 375°F.

COMBINE flour, baking soda, salt and cinnamon in small bowl. Beat butter, granulated sugar, brown sugar, eggs and vanilla extract in large mixer bowl. Gradually beat in flour mixture. Stir in oats and morsels. Drop by rounded tablespoonfuls onto ungreased baking sheets.

BAKE for 7 to 8 minutes for chewy cookies or 9 to 10 minutes for crispy cookies. Cool on baking sheets for 2 minutes; remove to wire racks to cool completely.

Makes about 4 dozen cookies

Pan Cookie Variation: GREASE 15×10-inch jelly-roll pan. Spread dough into prepared pan. Bake for 18 to 22 minutes or until light brown. Cool completely in pan on wire rack. Makes 4 dozen bars.

creamy lemon nut bars

½ cup (1 stick) butter or
   margarine, softened
⅓ cup powdered sugar
2 teaspoons vanilla
1¾ cups flour, divided
⅓ cup PLANTERS® Pecans,
   chopped

1 package (8 ounces)
   PHILADELPHIA®
   Cream Cheese, softened
2 cups granulated sugar
3 eggs
½ cup lemon juice
1 tablespoon grated lemon peel
1 tablespoon powdered sugar

PREHEAT oven to 350°F. Line 13×9-inch baking pan with foil; spray with cooking spray. Mix butter, ⅓ cup powdered sugar and vanilla in large bowl. Gradually stir in 1½ cups of the flour and pecans. Press dough firmly onto bottom of prepared pan. Bake 15 minutes.

BEAT cream cheese and granulated sugar in medium bowl with electric mixer on high speed until well blended. Add remaining ¼ cup flour and eggs; beat until blended.

STIR in lemon juice and peel. Pour over baked crust in pan. Bake 30 minutes or until set. Remove from oven; cool completely. Sprinkle with 1 tablespoon powdered sugar; cut into 32 bars. *Makes 32 servings (1 bar each)*

How To Grate Citrus Peel: Always wash and dry citrus fruit before grating. Move whole citrus fruit up and down on the side of the grater with the smallest holes to remove ONLY the surface of the fruit peel. (The inner white part is bitter.) Continue to grate fruit until you have the desired amount of grated peel, rotating fruit on the grater as necessary. Use this technique for grating any citrus fruit.

Substitute: Prepare as directed, using lime juice and grated lime peel.

Prep Time: 20 minutes plus cooling
Bake Time: 30 minutes

creamy lemon nut bars

"m&m's"® jam sandwiches

½ cup (1 stick) butter, softened
¾ cup granulated sugar
1 large egg
1 teaspoon almond extract
½ teaspoon vanilla extract
1⅓ cups all-purpose flour

¼ teaspoon baking powder
¼ teaspoon salt
Powdered sugar
½ cup seedless raspberry jam
½ cup "M&M's"® Chocolate
Mini Baking Bits

In large bowl cream butter and sugar until light and fluffy; beat in egg, almond extract and vanilla. In small bowl combine flour, baking powder and salt; blend into creamed mixture. Wrap and refrigerate dough 2 to 3 hours. Preheat oven to 375°F. Working with half the dough at a time on lightly floured surface, roll to ⅛-inch thickness. Cut into desired shapes using 3-inch cookie cutters. Cut out equal numbers of each shape. (If dough becomes too soft, refrigerate several minutes before continuing.) Cut 1½- to 2-inch centers out of half the cookies of each shape. Reroll trimmings and cut out more cookies. Using rigid spatula, carefully transfer shapes to ungreased cookie sheets. Bake 7 to 9 minutes. Cool on cookie sheets 1 to 2 minutes; cool completely on wire racks. Sprinkle powdered sugar on cookies with holes. Spread about 1 teaspoon jam on flat side of whole cookies, spreading almost to edges. Place cookies with holes, flat side down, over jam. Place "M&M's"® Chocolate Mini Baking Bits over jam in holes. Store between layers of waxed paper in tightly covered container.

Makes 1 dozen sandwich cookies

s'more cookie bars

¾ cup IMPERIAL® Spread,
melted
3 cups graham cracker crumbs
1 package (6 ounces) semisweet
chocolate chips (1 cup)

1 cup butterscotch chips
1 cup mini marshmallows
1 can (14 ounces) sweetened
condensed milk

1. Preheat oven to 350°F.

2. In 13×9-inch baking pan, combine Imperial® Spread with crumbs; press to form even layer. Evenly sprinkle with chocolate chips, then butterscotch chips, then mini marshmallows. Pour condensed milk evenly over mixture.

3. Bake 25 minutes or until bubbly. On wire rack, let cool completely. To serve, cut into squares. For easier cutting, refrigerate 1 hour. *Makes 2 dozen bars*

Prep Time: 10 minutes
Bake Time: 25 minutes

"m&m's"® jam sandwiches

o'henrietta bars

Cooking spray
½ cup (1 stick) butter or margarine, softened
½ cup packed brown sugar
½ cup KARO® Light or Dark Corn Syrup

1 teaspoon vanilla
3 cups quick oats, uncooked
½ cup (3 ounces) semisweet chocolate chips
¼ cup creamy peanut butter

1. Preheat oven to 350°F. Spray 8- or 9-inch square baking pan with cooking spray.

2. Beat butter, brown sugar, corn syrup and vanilla in large bowl with mixer at medium speed until smooth. Stir in oats. Press into prepared pan.

3. Bake 25 minutes or until center is barely firm. Cool on wire rack 5 minutes.

4. Sprinkle with chocolate chips; top with small spoonfuls of peanut butter. Let stand 5 minutes; spread peanut butter and chocolate over bars, swirling to marble.

5. Cool completely on wire rack before cutting. Cut into bars; refrigerate 15 minutes to set topping. *Makes 24 bars*

monster cookies

3 cups quick oats (not instant)
½ cup all-purpose flour
2 teaspoons baking soda
1 teaspoon SPICE ISLANDS® Ground Saigon Cinnamon
1 cup (2 sticks) butter or margarine, softened
1 cup packed brown sugar
1 cup granulated sugar

1½ cups creamy peanut butter
2 eggs
2 teaspoons SPICE ISLANDS® 100% Pure Bourbon Vanilla Extract
1 package (12 ounces) semisweet chocolate chips
1 cup candy-coated chocolate pieces
1 cup raisins (optional)

1. Combine oats, flour, baking soda and cinnamon in a medium bowl; set aside.

2. Cream butter and sugars with an electric mixer in a large mixing bowl. Add peanut butter and mix well. Mix in eggs and vanilla until well blended. Stir in oat mixture. Fold in chocolate chips, candies and raisins, if desired.

3. Drop by tablespoonfuls onto ungreased cookie sheet.

4. Bake in a preheated 350°F oven for 12 minutes. Cool slightly on cookie sheet; finish cooling on wire racks. *Makes about 5 dozen cookies*

o'henrietta bars

almond shortbread cookies with chocolate filling

¾ cup sliced almonds, toasted*
1 cup (2 sticks) butter or
   margarine, softened
¾ cup granulated sugar
3 egg yolks
¾ teaspoon almond extract
2 cups all-purpose flour

Chocolate Filling
   (recipe follows)
Powdered sugar (optional)

*To toast almonds: Heat oven to 350°F.
Spread almonds in thin layer in shallow
baking pan. Bake 8 to 10 minutes, stirring
occasionally, until light golden brown; cool.

1. Finely chop almonds; set aside.

2. Beat butter and granulated sugar in large bowl until creamy. Add egg yolks and almond extract; beat well. Gradually add flour, beating until well blended. Stir in almonds. Refrigerate dough 1 to 2 hours or until firm enough to handle.

3. Heat oven to 350°F. On well-floured surface, roll about ¼ of dough to about ⅛-inch thickness (keep remaining dough in refrigerator). Using 2-inch round cookie cutter, cut into equal number of rounds. Place on ungreased cookie sheet. Repeat with remaining dough.

4. Bake 8 to 10 minutes or until almost set. Cool slightly; remove from cookie sheet to wire rack. Cool completely. Spread about 1 measuring teaspoonful Chocolate Filling onto bottom of one cookie. Top with second cookie; gently press together. Repeat with remaining cookies. Allow to set, about 1 hour. Lightly sift powdered sugar over top of cookies, if desired. Cover; store at room temperature.

Makes about 44 sandwich cookies

Chocolate Filling: Combine 1 cup HERSHEY'S Milk Chocolate Chips** and ⅓ cup whipping cream in small saucepan. Stir constantly over low heat until mixture is smooth. Remove from heat. Cool about 20 minutes or until slightly thickened and spreadable. **HERSHEY'S SPECIAL DARK® Chocolate Chips or HERSHEY'S Semi-Sweet Chocolate Chips may also be used. Makes about 1 cup filling.

**almond shortbread cookies
with chocolate filling**

chunky pecan pie bars

Crust
1½ cups all-purpose flour
½ cup (1 stick) butter or margarine, softened
¼ cup packed brown sugar

Filling
3 large eggs
¾ cup corn syrup

¾ cup granulated sugar
2 tablespoons butter or margarine, melted
1 teaspoon vanilla extract
1¾ cups (11.5-ounce package) NESTLÉ® TOLL HOUSE® Semi-Sweet Chocolate Chunks
1½ cups coarsely chopped pecans

PREHEAT oven to 350°F. Grease 13×9-inch baking pan.

For Crust
BEAT flour, butter and brown sugar in small mixer bowl until crumbly. Press into prepared baking pan.

BAKE for 12 to 15 minutes or until lightly browned.

For Filling
BEAT eggs, corn syrup, granulated sugar, butter and vanilla extract in medium bowl with wire whisk. Stir in chunks and nuts. Pour evenly over baked crust.

BAKE for 25 to 30 minutes or until set. Cool completely in pan on wire rack. Cut into bars. *Makes 3 dozen bars*

mexican wedding cakes

1 cup (2 sticks) butter, softened
½ cup powdered sugar, plus additional for dusting cookies
2 teaspoons WATKINS® Vanilla
2 cups sifted all-purpose flour

1 cup finely chopped walnuts, almonds or pecans
2 tablespoons half-and-half
WATKINS® Ground Cinnamon

Preheat oven to 350°F. Beat butter, ½ cup sugar and vanilla in large bowl until light and fluffy. Stir in flour, walnuts and half-and-half; beat until smooth. Shape dough into 1-inch balls; place on ungreased cookie sheets.

Bake for 15 to 20 minutes or until set but not brown. Cool slightly; roll in powdered sugar to coat and set on wire racks to cool. Combine additional powdered sugar with cinnamon to taste. Roll cookies in cinnamon-sugar mixture. Store in airtight containers. *Makes 36 cookies*

chunky pecan pie bars

spiced raisin cookies with white chocolate drizzle

2 cups all-purpose flour	¾ cup butter, softened
1½ teaspoons ground cinnamon	¼ cup molasses
1 teaspoon baking soda	1 large egg
1 teaspoon ground ginger	1 cup SUN-MAID® Raisins or Golden Raisins
½ teaspoon ground allspice	4 ounces white chocolate, coarsely chopped
¼ teaspoon salt	
1 cup sugar	

HEAT oven to 375°F.

COMBINE flour, cinnamon, baking soda, ginger, allspice and salt in small bowl. Set aside.

BEAT sugar and butter in large bowl until light and fluffy.

ADD molasses and egg; beat well.

BEAT in raisins. Gradually beat in flour mixture on low speed just until incorporated.

DROP dough by tablespoonfuls onto ungreased cookie sheets 2 inches apart. Flatten dough slightly.

BAKE 12 to 14 minutes or until set. Cool on cookie sheets 1 minute; transfer to wire racks and cool completely.

MICROWAVE chocolate in heavy resealable plastic bag at high power 30 seconds. Turn bag over; heat additional 30 to 45 seconds or until almost melted. Knead bag with hands to melt remaining chocolate. Cut ⅛-inch corner off one end of bag. Drizzle cooled cookies with chocolate. Let stand until chocolate is set, about 20 minutes.

Makes about 2 dozen cookies

Prep Time: 15 minutes
Bake Time: 14 minutes

spiced raisin cookies with
white chocolate drizzle

caramel-topped cheesecake squares

1½ cups crushed NILLA® Wafers (about 50 wafers)

1 cup chopped PLANTERS® Pecans, divided

¼ cup (½ stick) butter, melted

4 packages (8 ounces each) PHILADELPHIA® Cream Cheese, softened

1 cup sugar

1 cup BREAKSTONE'S® or KNUDSEN® Sour Cream

3 tablespoons all-purpose flour

1 tablespoon vanilla

4 eggs

¼ cup caramel ice cream topping

PREHEAT oven to 325°F. Line 13×9-inch baking pan with foil, with ends of foil extending over sides of pan to form handles. Mix wafer crumbs, ½ cup of the pecans and the butter. Press firmly onto bottom of prepared pan. Refrigerate until needed.

BEAT cream cheese and sugar in large bowl with electric mixer on medium speed until well blended. Add sour cream, flour and vanilla; mix well. Add eggs, 1 at a time, mixing on low speed after each addition just until blended. Pour over crust.

BAKE 45 minutes or until center is almost set. Cool completely. Refrigerate 4 hours or overnight. Lift out of pan onto cutting board, using foil handles. Top with caramel topping and remaining ½ cup pecans. Let stand until topping is set. Store any leftovers in refrigerator.   *Makes 32 servings (1 square each)*

Prep Time: 15 minutes plus refrigerating
Bake Time: 45 minutes

domino® sugar cookies

1 cup DOMINO® Granulated Sugar

1 cup (2 sticks) butter or margarine, softened

1 egg

1 tablespoon vanilla

2¼ cups all-purpose flour

1 teaspoon baking soda

Additional DOMINO® Granulated Sugar

In large bowl, blend sugar and butter. Beat in egg and vanilla until light and fluffy. Mix in flour and baking soda. Divide dough in half. Shape each half into roll about 1½ inches in diameter. Wrap and refrigerate for 1 hour until chilled.* Cut rolls into ¼-inch slices. Place on ungreased baking sheet and sprinkle generously with additional sugar. Bake in 375°F oven for 10 to 12 minutes or until lightly browned around edges. Cool on wire rack.   *Makes about 3 dozen cookies*

To chill dough quickly, place in freezer for 30 minutes.

caramel-topped cheesecake squares

chocolate almond biscotti

1 package DUNCAN HINES®
  Moist Deluxe® Dark
  Chocolate Fudge Cake Mix
1 cup all-purpose flour
½ cup butter or margarine,
  melted

2 eggs
1 teaspoon almond extract
½ cup chopped almonds
  White chocolate, melted
  (optional)

1. Preheat oven to 350°F. Line 2 baking sheets with parchment paper.

2. Combine cake mix, flour, butter, eggs and almond extract in large bowl. Beat at low speed with electric mixer until well blended; stir in almonds. Divide dough in half. Shape each half into 12×2-inch log; place logs on prepared baking sheets.

3. Bake at 350°F for 30 to 35 minutes or until toothpick inserted into centers comes out clean. Remove logs from oven; cool on baking sheets 15 minutes. Using serrated knife, cut logs into ½-inch slices. Arrange slices on baking sheets. Bake biscotti 10 minutes. Remove to cooling racks; cool completely.

4. Dip one end of each biscotti into melted white chocolate, if desired. Allow white chocolate to set at room temperature before storing biscotti in airtight container.

Makes about 2½ dozen cookies

razzle-dazzle apple streusel bars

Crust and Streusel
2½ cups all-purpose flour
2 cups QUAKER® Oats (quick
  or old fashioned, uncooked)
1¼ cups granulated sugar
2 teaspoons baking powder
1 cup (2 sticks) margarine or
  butter, melted

Filling
3 cups peeled, thinly sliced
  apples (about 3 medium)
2 tablespoons all-purpose flour
1 (12-ounce) jar raspberry or
  apricot preserves

1. Heat oven to 375°F. For crust and streusel, combine flour, oats, sugar and baking powder; mix well. Add margarine, mixing until moistened. Reserve 2 cups; set aside. Press remaining oat mixture onto bottom of 13×9-inch baking pan. Bake 15 minutes.

2. For filling, combine apples and flour. Stir in preserves. Spread onto crust to within ½ inch of edges. Sprinkle with reserved oat mixture, pressing lightly. Bake 30 to 35 minutes or until light golden brown. Cool completely; cut into bars. Store tightly covered.

Makes 2 dozen bars

chocolate almond biscotti

mini kisses® blondies

1⅓ cups packed light brown sugar
½ cup (1 stick) butter or margarine, softened
2 eggs
2 teaspoons vanilla extract
¼ teaspoon salt

2 cups all-purpose flour
1½ teaspoons baking powder
1¾ cups (10-ounce package) HERSHEY'S MINI KISSES® Brand Milk Chocolates
½ cup chopped nuts

1. Heat oven to 350°F. Lightly grease 13×9×2-inch baking pan.

2. Beat brown sugar and butter in large bowl until fluffy. Add eggs, vanilla and salt; beat until blended. Add flour and baking powder; beat just until blended. Stir in chocolate pieces. Spread batter in prepared pan. Sprinkle nuts over top.

3. Bake 28 to 30 minutes or until set and golden brown. Cool completely in pan on wire rack. Cut into bars. *Makes about 36 bars*

thumbprint cookies

½ cup butter or margarine
¼ cup brown sugar, firmly packed
½ teaspoon vanilla extract
1 egg, separated

1 cup all-purpose flour
¼ teaspoon salt
¾ cup finely chopped nuts
1 (12-ounce) can SOLO® Date or Apricot Filling

Preheat oven to 375°F.

Cream butter or margarine, brown sugar and vanilla together. Stir in egg yolk and mix well. Stir in flour and salt. With lightly floured fingers, roll dough into balls about 1 inch in diameter. Beat egg white slightly. Dip cookie dough balls into egg white and roll in nuts.

Place on ungreased baking sheet. Press thumb into center of each cookie. Fill depression in cookie with desired filling. Bake 12 to 15 minutes or until lightly browned and set. Remove from baking sheet and cool on wire rack. Add more filling, if desired, before serving cookies. *Makes about 2 dozen cookies*

Tip: These cookies can be baked without filling and filled when they are cool. If you choose to follow this method, press depressions in cookies again when they are removed from the oven to allow enough room for the filling.

mini kisses® blondies

milk chocolate florentine cookies

⅔ cup butter
2 cups quick oats
1 cup granulated sugar
⅔ cup all-purpose flour
¼ cup light or dark corn syrup

¼ cup milk
1 teaspoon vanilla extract
¼ teaspoon salt
1¾ cups (11.5-ounce package)
NESTLÉ® TOLL HOUSE®
Milk Chocolate Morsels

PREHEAT oven to 375°F. Line baking sheets with foil.

MELT butter in medium saucepan; remove from heat. Stir in oats, sugar, flour, corn syrup, milk, vanilla extract and salt; mix well. Drop by level teaspoon, about 3 inches apart, onto prepared baking sheets. Spread thinly with rubber spatula.

BAKE for 6 to 8 minutes or until golden brown. Cool completely on baking sheets on wire racks. Peel foil from cookies.

MICROWAVE morsels in medium, uncovered, microwave-safe bowl on MEDIUM-HIGH (70%) power for 1 minute. Stir. Morsels may retain some of their original shape. If necessary, microwave at additional 10- to 15-second intervals, stirring just until morsels are melted. Spread thin layer of melted chocolate onto flat side of *half* the cookies. Top with *remaining* cookies. *Makes about 3½ dozen sandwich cookies*

ooey gooey krisper bars

1 cup KARO® Light or Dark
   Corn Syrup
1 cup granulated sugar
½ teaspoon salt
1 cup crunchy or creamy
   peanut butter

5 cups crispy rice or corn flakes
   cereal
1 cup semisweet chocolate chips
½ cup peanut butter chips
   (optional)

1. Combine corn syrup, sugar and salt in medium saucepan and cook over medium heat, stirring to dissolve sugar. (OR microwave on HIGH (100%) for 2 to 2½ minutes until syrup bubbles around the edge.)

2. Bring to a boil; add peanut butter and stir until blended. Remove from heat.

3. Stir in cereal. Pour into greased 13×9-inch pan; pat with greased spatula or waxed paper to level.

4. Melt chocolate chips in small saucepan over low heat, stirring constantly. (OR microwave on medium-high heat (70%) for 1 minute. Stir, then microwave at additional 10- to 20-second intervals, stirring until smooth.) Spread over bars. If desired, melt peanut butter chips and use small spoon to dot or drizzle onto bars in any design you prefer. Cool and cut into squares. *Makes 32 squares*

milk chocolate florentine cookies

frosted pumpkin squares

Cake

- ¾ cup (1½ sticks) butter or margarine
- 2 cups granulated sugar
- 1 can (16 ounces) pumpkin
- 4 eggs
- 2 cups flour
- 2 teaspoons CALUMET® Baking Powder
- 1 teaspoon ground cinnamon
- ½ teaspoon baking soda
- ½ teaspoon salt
- ¼ teaspoon ground nutmeg
- 1 cup chopped PLANTERS® Walnuts

Frosting

- 1 package (8 ounces) PHILADELPHIA® Cream Cheese, softened
- ⅓ cup butter or margarine
- 1 teaspoon vanilla
- 3 cups sifted powdered sugar

Cake

MIX butter and sugar with electric mixer on medium speed until light and fluffy. Blend in pumpkin and eggs. Mix in combined dry ingredients. Stir in walnuts.

SPREAD into greased and floured 15×10×1-inch baking pan.

BAKE at 350°F for 30 to 35 minutes or until wooden pick inserted in center comes out clean; cool.

Frosting

MIX cream cheese, butter and vanilla in large bowl with electric mixer until creamy. Gradually add sugar, mixing well after each addition. Spread onto cake. Cut into squares.

Makes 2 dozen squares

Make Ahead: Prepare recipe as directed, omitting frosting. Wrap securely; freeze. When ready to serve, thaw at room temperature. Frost, if desired.

Prep Time: 20 minutes
Bake Time: 35 minutes

frosted pumpkin square

chewy chocolate no-bakes

1 cup (6 ounces) semisweet
   chocolate chips
5 tablespoons light butter
14 large marshmallows
1 teaspoon vanilla

2 cups QUAKER® Oats (quick
   or old fashioned, uncooked)
⅔ cup (any combination of)
   raisins, diced dried mixed
   fruit, shredded coconut,
   miniature marshmallows
   or chopped nuts

1. Melt chocolate chips, butter and large marshmallows in large saucepan over low heat, stirring until smooth. Remove from heat; cool slightly. Stir in vanilla. Stir in oats and remaining ingredients.

2. Drop by rounded tablespoonfuls onto waxed paper. Cover and refrigerate 2 to 3 hours. Let stand at room temperature about 15 minutes before serving. Store, tightly covered, in refrigerator. *Makes about 36 treats*

Microwave Directions: Place chocolate chips, butter and marshmallows in large microwave-safe bowl. Microwave on HIGH (100% power) 1 to 2 minutes or until mixture is melted and smooth, stirring every 30 seconds. Proceed as directed.

classic peanut butter cookies

2½ cups all-purpose flour
1 teaspoon baking powder
1 teaspoon baking soda
¼ teaspoon salt
1 cup SKIPPY® Creamy
   or SUPER CHUNK®
   Peanut Butter

1 cup IMPERIAL® Spread,
   softened
1 cup granulated sugar
1 cup firmly packed brown sugar
2 eggs
1 teaspoon vanilla extract

1. Preheat oven to 350°F. Combine flour, baking powder, baking soda and salt in small bowl; set aside.

2. Beat Skippy® Creamy Peanut Butter with Imperial® Spread in large bowl with electric mixer until smooth. Beat in sugars, then eggs and vanilla until blended. Beat in flour mixture just until blended. (If necessary, refrigerate dough until easy to handle.)

3. Shape dough into 1-inch balls. Arrange balls on ungreased baking sheets 2 inches apart. Gently flatten each cookie and press crisscross pattern into tops with fork dipped in sugar.

4. Bake 12 minutes or until lightly golden. Cool completely on wire rack. Store in tightly covered container. *Makes 6 dozen cookies*

chewy chocolate no-bakes

peppermint pattie fudge bars

16 or 17 small (1½-inch) YORK®
Peppermint Patties, divided

1½ cups vanilla wafer crumbs
(about 45 wafers, crushed)

½ cup HERSHEY'S SPECIAL
DARK® Cocoa, divided

½ cup powdered sugar

¼ cup (½ stick) butter or
margarine, melted

1 can (14 ounces) sweetened
condensed milk (not
evaporated milk)

¼ cup all-purpose flour

1 egg

1 teaspoon vanilla extract

½ teaspoon baking powder

Additional powdered sugar

½ teaspoon water

1. Heat oven to 350°F. Unwrap and coarsely chop peppermint patties; set aside. Stir together cookie crumbs, ¼ cup cocoa, ½ cup powdered sugar and melted butter. Press firmly on bottom of ungreased 13×9×2-inch baking pan.

2. Beat sweetened condensed milk, flour, remaining ¼ cup cocoa, egg, vanilla and baking powder in large bowl until well blended. Spread evenly over prepared crust. Set aside 2 tablespoons peppermint pattie pieces; sprinkle remaining pieces over filling.

3. Bake 18 to 23 minutes or until set. Cool completely in pan on wire rack. Sprinkle cooled bars with additional powdered sugar.

4. Place reserved peppermint patties and water in small microwave-safe bowl. Microwave at MEDIUM (50%) 30 seconds; stir. If necessary, microwave an additional 10 seconds at a time, stirring after each heating, until patties are melted and smooth when stirred. Immediately drizzle over bars. Allow drizzle to set. Cut into bars. *Makes 36 bars*

tip: *To crush vanilla wafers into crumbs, use a food processor or place the cookies in a heavy resealable food storage bag and crush them with a rolling pin or meat mallet.*

peppermint pattie fudge bars

cakes
& cheesecakes

strawberry raspberry cake

1 package **DUNCAN HINES**®
   Moist Deluxe® Strawberry
   Supreme Cake Mix
2 ounces white chocolate baking
   bar, grated, divided

½ cup red raspberry jam
1 container **DUNCAN HINES**®
   Creamy Home-Style Classic
   Vanilla Frosting
Red raspberries (optional)

1. Preheat oven to 350°F. Grease and flour two 9-inch round cake pans.

2. Prepare cake mix as directed on package. Stir in ½ cup grated chocolate. Set aside remaining chocolate for garnish. Bake at 350°F for 28 to 31 minutes or until toothpick inserted in center comes out clean. Cool in pans 15 minutes. Invert onto cooling racks. Cool completely.

3. Place one cake layer on serving plate. Spread with jam. Top with second cake layer. Frost sides and top of cake with frosting. Garnish with remaining grated chocolate and raspberries. *Makes 12 to 16 servings*

reese's® marble cheesecake

Crumb Crust (recipe follows)

3 packages (8 ounces each)
cream cheese, softened

1 cup sugar, divided

½ cup dairy sour cream

1 tablespoon vanilla extract

3 eggs

3 tablespoons all-purpose flour

¼ cup HERSHEY'S® Cocoa

1 tablespoon vegetable oil

1⅓ cups REESE'S® Peanut Butter
Chips (reserved from crust)

¼ cup milk

1. Heat oven to 450°F. Prepare Crumb Crust.

2. Beat cream cheese, ¾ cup sugar, sour cream and vanilla in large bowl on medium speed of electric mixer until smooth. Add eggs and flour; beat until blended.

3. Beat cocoa, remaining ¼ cup sugar and oil with 1½ cups cheese mixture in medium bowl. Place 1⅓ cups peanut butter chips and milk in small microwave-safe bowl. Microwave at MEDIUM (50%) 30 seconds; stir. If necessary, microwave at MEDIUM an additional 15 seconds at a time, stirring after each heating, until chips are melted when stirred. Gradually add warm peanut butter mixture to remaining vanilla batter; beat on high speed 5 minutes.

4. Spoon peanut butter and chocolate mixtures alternately over prepared crust. Gently swirl with knife or spatula for marbled effect.

5. Bake 10 minutes.* Without opening oven door, decrease temperature to 250°F and continue to bake 30 minutes. Turn off oven; leave cheesecake in oven 30 minutes without opening door. Remove from oven to wire rack; with knife, loosen cake from side of pan. Cool completely; remove side of pan. Refrigerate until serving time. Cover; refrigerate leftover cheesecake. *Makes 12 servings*

Cheesecake is less likely to crack if baked in a water bath.

crumb crust

1⅔ cups (10-ounce package)
REESE'S® Peanut Butter
Chips, divided

1¼ cups vanilla wafer crumbs
(about 40 wafers, crushed)

¼ cup HERSHEY'S® Cocoa

¼ cup powdered sugar

¼ cup (½ stick) butter or
margarine, melted

With knife or food processor, chop ⅓ cup peanut butter chips (reserve remaining chips for cheesecake batter). Stir together crumbs, cocoa, powdered sugar and butter in medium bowl. Stir in chopped peanut butter chips. Press firmly onto bottom of 9-inch springform pan or 9-inch square pan.

reese's® marble cheesecake

tropical sunshine cake

1 package (18¼ ounces)
  yellow cake mix
1 can (12 fluid ounces)
  NESTLÉ® CARNATION®
  Evaporated Milk
2 large eggs

1 can (20 ounces) crushed
  pineapple in juice, drained
  (juice reserved), *divided*
½ cup chopped almonds
¾ cup sifted powdered sugar
1 cup flaked coconut, toasted
  Whipped cream

PREHEAT oven to 350°F. Grease 13×9-inch baking pan.

COMBINE cake mix, evaporated milk and eggs in large mixer bowl. Beat on low speed for 2 minutes. Stir in *1 cup* pineapple. Pour batter into prepared baking pan. Sprinkle with almonds.

BAKE for 30 to 35 minutes or until wooden pick inserted in center comes out clean. Cool in pan on wire rack for 15 minutes.

COMBINE sugar and 2 tablespoons *reserved* pineapple juice in small bowl; mix until smooth. Spread over warm cake; sprinkle with coconut and *remaining* pineapple. Cool completely before serving. Top with whipped cream.   *Makes 12 servings*

mini pumpkin cheesecakes

18 (2½-inch) paper baking cups
18 gingersnap cookies
12 ounces cream cheese, softened
¾ cup sugar
1 tablespoon ARGO®
  Corn Starch

1 teaspoon SPICE ISLANDS®
  Pumpkin Pie Spice
2 eggs
1 cup canned pumpkin
⅓ cup KARO® Lite Syrup

1. Preheat oven to 325°F.

2. Line muffin pans with 18 paper baking cups. Place 1 gingersnap in each.

3. Beat cream cheese, sugar, corn starch and pumpkin pie spice with an electric mixer. Add eggs and mix well. Add pumpkin and syrup; beat 1 minute.

4. Pour filling into paper baking cups, dividing evenly. Bake in a preheated 325°F oven for 30 to 35 minutes, until just set.

5. Chill for 1 hour. Garnish as desired.   *Makes 18 servings*

Prep Time: 15 minutes
Bake Time: 30 to 35 minutes
Chill Time: 1 hour

tropical sunshine cake

philadelphia® classic cheesecake

1½ cups HONEY MAID®
   Graham Cracker Crumbs

3 tablespoons sugar

⅓ cup butter or margarine,
   melted

4 packages (8 ounces each)
   PHILADELPHIA®
   Cream Cheese, softened

1 cup sugar

1 teaspoon vanilla

4 eggs

PREHEAT oven to 325°F if using a silver 9-inch springform pan (or to 300°F if using a dark nonstick springform pan). Mix crumbs, 3 tablespoons sugar and butter; press firmly onto bottom of pan.

BEAT cream cheese, 1 cup sugar and vanilla with electric mixer on medium speed until well blended. Add eggs, 1 at a time, mixing on low speed after each addition just until blended. Pour over crust.

BAKE 55 minutes or until center is almost set. Loosen cake from side of pan; cool before removing side of pan. Refrigerate 4 hours or overnight. Store leftover cheesecake in refrigerator.   *Makes 16 servings*

Special Extra: Top with fresh fruit just before serving.

little banana upside down cakes

3 tablespoons margarine, melted

3 tablespoons flaked coconut,
   toasted

3 tablespoons chopped almonds,
   toasted

2 tablespoons brown sugar

1 firm, large DOLE® Banana,
   sliced

¼ cup cake flour

¼ teaspoon baking powder
   Pinch salt

1 egg

3 tablespoons granulated sugar

1 teaspoon rum extract

DIVIDE margarine, coconut, almonds, brown sugar and banana among 3 (¾-cup) soufflé dishes.

COMBINE flour, baking powder and salt.

BEAT egg and granulated sugar until thick and pale. Beat in rum extract. Fold in flour mixture. Pour batter evenly into prepared dishes.

BAKE at 350°F 15 to 20 minutes. Invert onto serving plates.   *Makes 3 servings*

philadelphia® classic cheesecake

sour cream chocolate cake

½ cup HERSHEY'S Cocoa

½ cup hot water

½ cup (1 stick) butter or margarine, softened

1 cup granulated sugar

½ cup packed light brown sugar

1½ teaspoons vanilla extract

3 eggs

1¾ cups all-purpose flour

1½ teaspoons baking powder

1 teaspoon baking soda

1 teaspoon salt

1 cup (8 ounces) dairy sour cream

Quick Fudge Frosting (recipe follows)

1. Heat oven to 350°F. Grease and flour two 9-inch round baking pans.

2. Combine cocoa and water in small bowl; stir until smooth. Set aside.

3. Beat butter in large bowl until creamy. Add granulated sugar, brown sugar and vanilla; beat until fluffy. Add eggs; beat well. Stir in cocoa mixture. Stir together flour, baking powder, baking soda and salt; add alternately with sour cream to butter mixture, beating just until blended. Pour batter into prepared pans.

4. Bake 30 to 35 minutes or until wooden pick inserted in center comes out clean. Cool 15 minutes; remove from pans to wire racks. Cool completely. Frost with Quick Fudge Frosting.   *Makes 8 to 10 servings*

quick fudge frosting

6 to 7 tablespoons light cream or evaporated milk

⅓ cup butter or margarine, softened

3 cups powdered sugar

6 tablespoons HERSHEY'S Cocoa

⅛ teaspoon salt

1 teaspoon vanilla extract

1. Heat cream in small saucepan until bubbles form around edge of pan; remove from heat and set aside.

2. Beat butter in medium bowl until creamy. Stir together powdered sugar, cocoa and salt; add alternately with cream to butter, beating to spreading consistency. Stir in vanilla.   *Makes about 2 cups frosting*

sour cream chocolate cake

milano® cookie caramel ice cream cake

1 package (6 ounces)
PEPPERIDGE FARM®
Milano® Cookies

3 cups vanilla or chocolate ice
cream, softened
⅓ cup prepared caramel topping

1. Line an 8-inch round cake pan with plastic wrap.

2. Cut the cookies in half crosswise and arrange around the edge of the pan. Place the remaining cookies into the bottom of the pan.

3. Spread 1½ **cups** ice cream over the cookies. Drizzle with the caramel topping. Spread the remaining ice cream over the caramel topping. Cover and freeze for 6 hours or until the ice cream is firm.

4. Uncover the pan and invert the cake onto a serving plate. Serve with additional caramel topping.   *Makes 8 servings*

Kitchen Tip: Substitute chocolate topping for the caramel topping.

Prep Time: 20 minutes
Freeze Time: 6 hours
Total Time: 6 hours 20 minutes

peppery poundcake

1 cup (2 sticks) butter or
margarine
1 cup granulated sugar
1 cup packed light brown sugar
4 eggs
3 cups sifted cake flour
2 teaspoons baking powder

½ teaspoon allspice
¼ teaspoon salt
1 cup milk
3 teaspoons vanilla extract
½ teaspoon Original TABASCO®
brand Pepper Sauce
Confectioners' sugar (optional)

Preheat oven to 350°F. Grease 9-inch tube pan. Beat butter, granulated and brown sugars in medium bowl until light and fluffy. Add eggs, one at a time, beating well after each addition.

Sift flour, baking powder, allspice and salt into medium bowl. Beat flour mixture and milk alternately into butter mixture; beat in vanilla and TABASCO® Sauce. Pour into prepared pan. Bake 50 to 60 minutes or until cake tester inserted near center comes out clean. Cool in pan on wire rack 20 to 30 minutes; remove from pan and cool completely. Before serving, dust with confectioners' sugar, if desired.   *Makes 8 to 10 servings*

double chocolate chip mini cheesecakes

1½ cups NESTLÉ® TOLL HOUSE® Refrigerated Chocolate Chip Cookie Tub Dough or 1 package (16.5 ounces) NESTLÉ® TOLL HOUSE® Refrigerated Chocolate Chip Cookie Bar Dough

2 packages (8 ounces *each*) cream cheese, at room temperature

¾ cup granulated sugar

2 tablespoons all-purpose flour

2 large eggs

1 teaspoon vanilla extract

¾ cup NESTLÉ® TOLL HOUSE® Semi-Sweet Chocolate Mini Morsels, *divided*

PREHEAT oven to 325°F. Paper-line 24 muffin cups. Place 1 level tablespoon of cookie dough (1 square if using bar dough) into each muffin cup.

BAKE for 10 minutes or until cookie has spread to edge of cup.

BEAT cream cheese, sugar and flour in large mixer bowl until creamy. Add eggs and vanilla extract; mix well. Stir *½ cup* morsels into batter. Spoon 2 heaping measuring tablespoons of batter over each cookie in cup.

BAKE for additional 13 to 15 minutes or until just set but not browned. Remove from oven to wire rack. Cool completely in pans on wire rack. Refrigerate for 1 hour.

MELT *remaining ¼ cup* mini morsels in small, heavy-duty plastic bag on HIGH (100%) power for 30 seconds; knead. Microwave at additional 10- to 15-second intervals, kneading until smooth. Cut tiny corner from bag; squeeze to drizzle lightly over each cheesecake just before serving. *Makes 24 servings*

Prep Time: 20 minutes
Bake Time: 23 minutes
Cool Time: 1 hour refrigerating

double chocolate chip mini cheesecakes

spicy applesauce cake

2¼ cups all-purpose flour
2 teaspoons baking soda
1 teaspoon ground cinnamon
1 teaspoon ground nutmeg
½ teaspoon ground cloves
1 cup firmly packed brown sugar

½ cup FILIPPO BERIO®
Extra Light Olive Oil,
plus some for the pan
1½ cups applesauce
1 cup raisins
1 cup coarsely chopped walnuts
Powdered sugar or sweetened
whipped cream (optional)

Preheat oven to 375°F. Grease 9-inch square pan with olive oil. In medium bowl, combine flour, baking soda, cinnamon, nutmeg and cloves.

In large bowl, mix brown sugar and olive oil with electric mixer at medium speed until blended. Add applesauce; mix well. Add flour mixture all at once; beat at low speed until well blended. Stir in raisins and nuts. Spoon batter into prepared pan.

Bake 20 to 25 minutes or until lightly browned. Cool completely on wire rack. Cut into squares. Serve plain, dusted with powdered sugar or frosted with whipped cream, if desired. *Makes 9 servings*

boston cream pie

1 package (3.4 ounces) JELL-O®
Vanilla Flavor Instant
Pudding
1 cup cold milk
1½ cups thawed COOL WHIP®
Whipped Topping

1 round yellow cake layer
(8- or 9-inch)
1 square BAKER'S®
Unsweetened Chocolate
1 tablespoon butter
¾ cup powdered sugar
2 tablespoons cold milk

BEAT pudding mix and 1 cup milk with whisk 2 minutes. Stir in COOL WHIP®. Let stand 5 minutes. Meanwhile, cut cake horizontally into 2 layers with serrated knife.

STACK cake layers on serving plate, spreading pudding mixture between layers.

MICROWAVE chocolate and butter in medium microwavable bowl on HIGH 1 minute; stir until chocolate is melted. Add sugar and 2 tablespoons milk; mix well. Spread over cake. Refrigerate 1 hour. *Makes 10 servings*

How To Slice Cake Layer Evenly: Place cooled cake layer on serving plate. Make a 2-inch horizontal cut around side of cake using a long serrated knife. Then, cut all of the way through the cake layer to make 2 layers.

spicy applesauce cake

simply sensational strawberry cake

Nonstick cooking spray
3 cups all-purpose flour
2 teaspoons baking powder
1 teaspoon baking soda
1 cup sugar
⅓ cup butter, softened

¾ cup cholesterol-free egg substitute, beaten
1 cup plain fat-free yogurt
1½ cups POLANER® Sugar Free Strawberry or Sugar Free Peach Preserves, divided

Heat oven to 350°F. Lightly coat 10-inch fluted tube pan with cooking spray.

Combine flour, baking powder and baking soda in medium bowl; set aside.

Beat sugar and butter in large mixer bowl until blended. Beat in egg substitute until well blended. Alternately add flour mixture and yogurt, beating after each addition until well blended.

Spoon 1 cup preserves onto batter; gently fold, swirling preserves into batter. Pour batter into prepared pan.

Bake 45 to 50 minutes until wooden pick inserted near center comes out clean.

Cool in pan on wire rack 15 minutes. Remove from pan to rack to cool completely.

Microwave remaining ½ cup preserves on HIGH 30 to 45 seconds, stirring as needed, until melted. Drizzle over cooled cake. *Makes 16 servings (1 slice per serving)*

Tips: If the preserves seem too thick to drizzle easily, stir in water, 1 teaspoon at a time, to desired consistency. For a special touch, add a dollop of light whipped topping and a fresh strawberry to each slice of cake.

Prep Time: 15 minutes
Bake Time: 45 minutes
Cool Time: 30 minutes

philadelphia® chocolate-vanilla swirl cheesecake

20 **OREO®** Chocolate Sandwich
    Cookies, crushed
    (about 2 cups)

3 tablespoons butter, melted

4 packages (8 ounces each)
    PHILADELPHIA®
    Cream Cheese, softened

1 cup sugar

1 teaspoon vanilla

1 cup **BREAKSTONE'S®** or
    KNUDSEN® Sour Cream

4 eggs

6 squares **BAKER'S®**
    Semi-Sweet Baking
    Chocolate, melted, cooled

HEAT oven to 325°F. Mix cookie crumbs and butter. Press firmly onto bottom of foil-lined 13×9-inch baking pan. Bake 10 minutes.

BEAT cream cheese, sugar and vanilla in large bowl with electric mixer on medium speed until well blended. Add sour cream; mix well. Add eggs, 1 at a time, beating on low speed after each addition just until blended. Remove 1 cup of the batter; set aside. Stir melted chocolate into remaining batter. Pour chocolate batter over crust; top with spoonfuls of remaining plain batter. Cut through batters with knife several times for swirled effect.

BAKE 40 minutes or until center is almost set. Cool. Refrigerate at least 4 hours or overnight. Store any leftover cheesecake in refrigerator. *Makes 16 servings*

Jazz It Up: Garnish with chocolate curls just before serving. Use a vegetable peeler to shave the side of an additional square of BAKER'S® Semi-Sweet Baking Chocolate and a square of BAKER'S® Premium White Baking Chocolate until desired amount of curls are obtained. Wrap remaining chocolate and store at room temperature for another use.

Prep Time: 15 minutes plus refrigerating
Bake Time: 40 minutes

philadelphia® chocolate-vanilla
swirl cheesecake

tomato soup spice cake

2 cups all-purpose flour
1⅓ cups sugar
4 teaspoons baking powder
1½ teaspoons ground allspice
1 teaspoon baking soda
1 teaspoon ground cinnamon
½ teaspoon ground cloves

1 can (10¾ ounces)
CAMPBELL'S®
Condensed Tomato Soup
½ cup vegetable shortening
2 eggs
¼ cup water
Cream Cheese Frosting
(recipe follows)

1. Heat the oven to 350°F. Grease 2 (8- or 9-inch) cake pans.

2. Stir the flour, sugar, baking powder, allspice, baking soda, cinnamon and cloves in a large bowl. Add the soup, shortening, eggs and water. Beat with an electric mixer on low speed just until blended. Increase the speed to high and beat for 4 minutes. Pour the batter into the pans.

3. Bake for 40 minutes or until a toothpick inserted in the centers comes out clean. Let the cakes cool in the pans on wire racks for 20 minutes. Frost with the Cream Cheese Frosting.   *Makes 12 servings*

Cream Cheese Frosting: Beat **1 package** (8 ounces) cream cheese, softened, **2 tablespoons** milk and **1 teaspoon** vanilla extract in a medium bowl with an electric mixer on medium speed until the mixture is creamy. Slowly beat in **1 package** (16 ounces) confectioners' sugar until the frosting is desired consistency.

Kitchen Tip: The cake can also be prepared in a 13×9-inch baking pan.

Prep Time: 20 minutes
Bake Time: 40 minutes
Cool Time: 20 minutes

tomato soup spice cake

nutty toffee coffee cake

1⅓ cups (8-ounce package) HEATH® BITS 'O BRICKLE® Toffee Bits, divided

⅓ cup plus ¾ cup packed light brown sugar, divided

2¼ cups all-purpose flour, divided

9 tablespoons butter or margarine, softened and divided

¾ cup granulated sugar

2 teaspoons baking powder

½ teaspoon ground cinnamon

¼ teaspoon salt

1¼ cups milk

1 egg

1 teaspoon vanilla extract

¾ cup chopped nuts

1. Heat oven to 350°F. Grease and flour 13×9×2-inch baking pan. Stir together ½ cup toffee bits, ⅓ cup brown sugar, ¼ cup flour and 3 tablespoons butter. Stir until crumbly; set aside.

2. Combine remaining 2 cups flour, granulated sugar, remaining ¾ cup brown sugar, remaining 6 tablespoons butter, baking powder, cinnamon and salt in large mixer bowl; mix until well blended. Gradually add milk, egg and vanilla, beating until thoroughly blended. Stir in remaining toffee bits and nuts. Spread batter in prepared pan.

3. Sprinkle reserved crumb topping over batter. Bake 30 to 35 minutes or until wooden pick inserted in center comes out clean. Serve warm or cool.

Makes 12 to 16 servings

spiced gingerbread

1½ cups bran flakes

1 cup milk

1½ cups all-purpose flour

2 teaspoons baking soda

1 teaspoon ground cinnamon

1 teaspoon ground ginger

½ teaspoon ground cloves

1 cup GRANDMA'S® Molasses

½ cup butter, melted

3 eggs

Confectioners' sugar (optional)

Heat oven to 350°F. In large bowl, mix bran flakes and milk; let stand 5 minutes. In separate bowl, mix flour, baking soda, cinnamon, ginger and cloves; set aside. In another bowl, with electric mixer at medium speed, beat molasses, butter and eggs until smooth. Blend in bran and flour mixtures. Pour batter into greased and floured 13×9×2-inch baking pan.

Bake 40 to 45 minutes or until toothpick inserted in center comes out clean. Cool in pan 10 minutes. Remove from pan; cool completely on wire rack. Sprinkle with confectioners' sugar, if desired; cut into 2½×2-inch pieces. *Makes 20 servings*

philly® blueberry swirl cheesecake

1 cup HONEY MAID®
  Graham Cracker Crumbs

1 cup plus 3 tablespoons sugar,
  divided

3 tablespoons butter or
  margarine, melted

4 packages (8 ounces each)
  PHILADELPHIA®
  Cream Cheese, softened

1 teaspoon vanilla

1 cup BREAKSTONE'S® or
  KNUDSEN® Sour Cream

4 eggs

2 cups fresh or thawed frozen
  blueberries

HEAT oven to 325°F. Mix crumbs, 3 tablespoons of the sugar and butter. Press firmly onto bottom of foil-lined 13×9-inch baking pan. Bake 10 minutes.

BEAT cream cheese, remaining 1 cup sugar and vanilla in large bowl with electric mixer on medium speed until well blended. Add sour cream; mix well. Add eggs, 1 at a time, beating on low speed after each addition just until blended. Pour over crust. Purée blueberries in a blender or food processor. Gently drop spoonfuls of puréed blueberries over batter; cut through batter several times with knife for marble effect.

BAKE 45 minutes or until center is almost set; cool. Cover and refrigerate at least 4 hours before serving. Store leftover cheesecake in refrigerator. *Makes 16 servings*

Substitution: Substitute 1 can (15 ounces) blueberries, well drained, for the 2 cups fresh or frozen blueberries.

Make It Easy: Instead of using a blender, crush the blueberries in a bowl with a fork. Drain before spooning over the cheesecake batter and swirling to marbleize as directed.

Prep Time: 15 minutes
Bake Time: 45 minutes

philly® blueberry swirl cheesecake

hummingbird cake

1 package DUNCAN HINES®
Moist Deluxe® Classic
Yellow Cake Mix

1 package (4-serving size)
vanilla-flavor instant
pudding and pie filling mix

½ cup vegetable oil

1 can (8 ounces) crushed
pineapple, well drained
(reserve juice)

Reserved pineapple juice
plus water to equal 1 cup

4 eggs

1 teaspoon ground cinnamon

½ medium-size ripe banana,
cut up

½ cup finely chopped pecans

¼ cup chopped maraschino
cherries, well drained

Confectioners' sugar

1. Preheat oven to 350°F. Grease and flour 10-inch bundt or tube pan.

2. Combine cake mix, pudding mix, oil, pineapple, 1 cup juice and water mixture, eggs and cinnamon in large bowl. Beat at low speed with electric mixer until moistened. Beat at medium speed 2 minutes. Stir in banana, pecans and cherries. Pour into pan. Bake at 350°F 50 to 60 minutes or until toothpick inserted near center comes out clean. Cool in pan 25 minutes. Invert onto serving plate. Sprinkle with confectioners' sugar.

Makes 12 to 16 servings

Tip: Also great with Cream Cheese Glaze. For glaze, heat 1 container DUNCAN HINES® Creamy Home-Style Cream Cheese Frosting in microwave at HIGH (100% power) 30 seconds. Do not overheat. Stir until smooth. Drizzle over cake.

lemon loaf cake

2 cups sifted cake flour

½ teaspoon ARM & HAMMER®
Baking Soda

¼ teaspoon salt

½ cup butter or margarine

1 cup sugar

2 eggs

½ cup milk

4½ teaspoons lemon juice

1 teaspoon grated lemon peel

Sift together flour, Baking Soda and salt. Beat butter in large bowl with electric mixer until light and fluffy. Add sugar gradually, beating after each addition. In separate bowl, beat eggs until thick and lemon colored. Slowly beat eggs into butter mixture. Combine milk and lemon juice; add alternately to batter with flour mixture. After each addition, beat until smooth. Stir in lemon peel. Turn into greased and floured 8-inch square pan. Bake at 350°F 45 minutes or until toothpick inserted in center comes out clean. Cool in pan 10 minutes. Remove from pan and cool on wire rack.

Makes 16 servings

hummingbird cake

classic desserts

rayna's nutty marshmallow-topped chocolate cupcakes

1 box (18 ounces) chocolate cake mix	½ cup **SKIPPY®** Creamy Peanut Butter
1 cup **HELLMANN'S®** or **BEST FOODS®** Real Mayonnaise	2 jars (7½ ounces each) marshmallow creme
1 cup water	1 cup frozen whipped topping, thawed
3 eggs	Chocolate sprinkles or other cake decorations (optional)

1. Preheat oven to 350°F. Line two 12-cup muffin pans with cupcake liners; set aside.

2. Beat cake mix, Hellmann's® or Best Foods® Real Mayonnaise, water and eggs in large bowl with electric mixer on low speed 30 seconds. Beat on medium speed, scraping sides occasionally, 2 minutes. Evenly pour into prepared pans.

3. Bake 18 minutes or until toothpick inserted in centers comes out clean. Cool 10 minutes on wire racks; remove from pans and cool completely.

4. Meanwhile, whisk together Skippy® Creamy Peanut Butter, marshmallow creme and whipped topping in medium bowl. Frost cupcakes with peanut butter frosting. Decorate as desired. *Makes 24 servings*

Tip: Cake batter can also be baked in two 9-inch or one 13×9-inch cake pan and then frosted.

Prep Time: 15 minutes
Bake Time: 18 minutes

best-ever baked rice pudding

3 eggs
⅓ cup sugar
¼ teaspoon salt
2 cups milk
2 cups *cooked* rice

½ cup golden raisins
Grated peel of 1 SUNKIST® lemon
Warm Lemon Sauce (recipe follows)

In bowl, beat eggs lightly with sugar and salt. Stir in milk, rice, raisins and lemon peel. Pour into well-buttered 1-quart casserole. Bake, uncovered, at 325°F 50 to 60 minutes or until set. Serve with Warm Lemon Sauce. Refrigerate leftovers.

Makes 6 servings (about 3½ cups)

warm lemon sauce

⅓ cup sugar
2 tablespoons cornstarch
⅛ teaspoon salt
Dash nutmeg (optional)
¾ cup water

Grated peel of ½ SUNKIST® lemon
Juice of 1 SUNKIST® lemon
1 tablespoon butter or margarine
Few drops yellow food coloring (optional)

In small saucepan, combine sugar, cornstarch, salt and nutmeg. Gradually blend in water, lemon peel and juice. Add butter. Cook over medium heat, stirring until thickened. Stir in food coloring. Serve warm.

Makes about 1 cup

tip: *When using both the peel and juice of a lemon, grate the peel first and then squeeze the juice. A medium lemon will yield 1 to 2 teaspoons grated peel and about 3 tablespoons juice.*

mini libby's® famous pumpkin pies

4 (1-cup volume *each*) 4-inch diameter mini-pie shells

¾ cup granulated sugar

1 teaspoon ground cinnamon

½ teaspoon salt

½ teaspoon ground ginger

¼ teaspoon ground cloves

2 large eggs

1 can (15 ounces) LIBBY'S® 100% Pure Pumpkin

1 can (12 fluid ounces) NESTLÉ® CARNATION® Evaporated Milk

PREHEAT oven to 425°F.

MIX sugar, cinnamon, salt, ginger and cloves in small bowl. Beat eggs lightly in large bowl. Stir in pumpkin and sugar-spice mixture. Gradually stir in evaporated milk.

POUR into shells.

BAKE for 15 minutes. Reduce oven temperature to 350°F; bake for 30 to 35 minutes or until knife inserted near center comes out clean. Cool on wire rack for 2 hours. Serve immediately or refrigerate. (Do not freeze as this may cause filling to separate from the crust.) *Makes 4 mini pies*

Note: May use refrigerated or homemade single pie crust to make 4 mini-pie shells. Lay rim of mini-pie pan on rolled out dough. Cut circle ½ inch larger than mini-pie to allow for dough to form fluted edge.

For Lower Fat/Calories Pies: Substitute NESTLÉ® CARNATION® Lowfat Evaporated or Fat Free Evaporated Milk.

Prep Time: 8 minutes
Bake Time: 45 minutes
Cool Time: 2 hours

apple strudel

1 egg

1 tablespoon water

2 tablespoons granulated sugar

1 tablespoon all-purpose flour

¼ teaspoon ground cinnamon

2 large Granny Smith apples, peeled, cored and thinly sliced

2 tablespoons raisins

½ of a 17.3-ounce package PEPPERIDGE FARM® Puff Pastry Sheets (1 sheet), thawed

Confectioners' sugar (optional)

1. Heat the oven to 375°F. Beat the egg and water in a small bowl with a fork or whisk. Stir the granulated sugar, flour and cinnamon in a medium bowl. Add the apples and raisins and toss to coat.

2. Unfold the pastry sheet on a lightly floured surface. Roll the pastry sheet into a 16×12-inch rectangle. With the short side facing you, spoon the apple mixture onto the bottom half of the pastry sheet to within 1 inch of the edge. Roll up like a jelly roll. Place seam-side down onto a baking sheet. Tuck the ends under to seal. Brush the pastry with the egg mixture. Cut several slits in the top of the pastry.

3. Bake for 35 minutes or until the strudel is golden brown. Let the strudel cool on the baking sheet on a wire rack for 20 minutes. Sprinkle with the confectioners' sugar, if desired. *Makes 6 servings*

Kitchen Tip: Make sure to toss the apples and raisins until they're evenly coated with the flour mixture. The flour helps to thicken the juices released by the apples as they cook.

white chocolate mousse

1 cup white chocolate chips *or* 7 ounces white chocolate, chopped

¼ cup hot water

2 teaspoons WATKINS® Vanilla

2 cups heavy whipping cream

½ cup sifted powdered sugar

Melt chips in top of double boiler or in microwave. Add hot water and vanilla; mix until smooth. Cool completely. Beat cream until it begins to thicken. Add sugar; continue beating until soft peaks form. Stir large spoonful of whipped cream into chip mixture, then fold mixture back into remaining whipped cream. Spoon mousse into individual custard cups or 4-cup mold. Refrigerate until thoroughly chilled. Serve cold. *Makes 8 servings*

apple strudel

creamy strawberry cookie "tarts"

⅔ cup boiling water

1 package (4-serving size) JELL-O® Strawberry Flavor Gelatin

1 package (8 ounces) PHILADELPHIA® Cream Cheese, cubed

1 cup thawed COOL WHIP® Whipped Topping

12 CHIPS AHOY!® Real Chocolate Chip Cookies

12 small strawberries

STIR boiling water into dry gelatin mix in small bowl at least 2 minutes until completely dissolved. Cool 5 minutes, stirring occasionally.

POUR gelatin mixture into blender. Add cream cheese; cover. Blend on medium speed 30 to 45 seconds or until well blended; scrape down side of blender container, if needed. Add whipped topping; cover. Blend on low speed 5 seconds or just until blended.

LINE 12 muffin pan cups with paper liners; spray with cooking spray. Place 1 cookie on bottom of each prepared cup; top evenly with the gelatin mixture. Refrigerate 1 hour 30 minutes or until firm. Top each with a strawberry just before serving. Store leftover desserts in refrigerator. *Makes 12 servings*

Prep Time: 15 minutes plus refrigerating

cherries jubilee

2 (16-ounce) cans dark sweet cherries

¼ cup granulated sugar

2 teaspoons cornstarch

1 tablespoon grated orange peel

½ cup brandy or cognac, optional

1 pound cake, cut into 16 slices, or 1-quart vanilla ice cream

Drain cherries, reserving syrup. Combine cherry syrup with sugar and cornstarch in a chafing dish or electric skillet. Cook, stirring constantly, over medium heat about 5 minutes, or until smooth and clear. Add cherries and orange peel; heat thoroughly.

Gently heat brandy or cognac in a small saucepan; pour over heated cherries. Flame, if desired. Stir gently and ladle over pound cake or ice cream. *Makes 8 servings*

Favorite recipe from **Cherry Marketing Institute**

cranberry apple crisp

Filling

½ cup granulated sugar

3 tablespoons ARGO® or KINGSFORD'S® Corn Starch

1 teaspoon SPICE ISLANDS® Ground Saigon Cinnamon

½ teaspoon SPICE ISLANDS® Ground Nutmeg

5 to 6 cups peeled, cubed tart apples

1 cup fresh or frozen cranberries

½ cup KARO® Light Corn Syrup

1 teaspoon grated orange peel

Topping

½ cup walnuts or quick oats (not instant)

⅓ cup packed brown sugar

¼ cup all-purpose flour

¼ cup (½ stick) margarine or butter

1. Mix granulated sugar, corn starch, cinnamon and nutmeg in a large bowl. Add apples, cranberries, corn syrup and orange peel; toss to combine. Spoon into shallow 2-quart baking dish.

2. Combine walnuts, brown sugar and flour in a small bowl. With a pastry blender or 2 knives, cut in butter until crumbly.

3. Top apple filling with walnut mixture.

4. Bake at 350°F for 50 minutes or until cranberries and apples are tender and juices that bubble up in center are shiny and clear. Cool slightly; serve warm.

Makes 8 servings

Prep Time: 25 minutes
Bake Time: 50 minutes

peanut butter and chocolate mousse pie

1⅔ cups (10-ounce package) REESE'S® Peanut Butter Chips, divided

1 package (3 ounces) cream cheese, softened

¼ cup powdered sugar

⅓ cup plus 2 tablespoons milk, divided

1 (9-inch) pie crust, baked and cooled

1 teaspoon unflavored gelatin

1 tablespoon cold water

2 tablespoons boiling water

½ cup granulated sugar

⅓ cup HERSHEY'S Cocoa

1 cup (½ pint) cold whipping cream

1 teaspoon vanilla extract

1. Melt 1½ cups peanut butter chips. Beat cream cheese, powdered sugar and ⅓ cup milk in medium bowl until smooth. Add melted chips; beat well. Beat in remaining 2 tablespoons milk. Spread in cooled crust.

2. Sprinkle gelatin over cold water in small bowl; let stand 1 minute to soften. Add boiling water; stir until gelatin is completely dissolved. Cool slightly. Combine granulated sugar and cocoa in medium bowl; add whipping cream and vanilla. Beat on medium speed of mixer until stiff; pour in gelatin mixture, beating until well blended. Spoon into crust over peanut butter layer. Refrigerate several hours. Garnish with remaining chips. Cover; refrigerate leftover pie. *Makes 6 to 8 servings*

ambrosia

1 can (20 ounces) DOLE® Pineapple Chunks, drained or 2 cups DOLE® Frozen Tropical Gold Pineapple Chunks, partially thawed

1 can (11 or 15 ounces) DOLE® Mandarin Oranges, drained

1 DOLE® Banana, sliced

1½ cups seedless grapes

½ cup miniature marshmallows

1 cup vanilla low fat yogurt

¼ cup flaked coconut, toasted

COMBINE pineapple chunks, mandarin oranges, banana, grapes and marshmallows in medium bowl.

STIR yogurt into fruit mixture. Sprinkle with coconut. *Makes 4 to 6 servings*

peanut butter and chocolate mousse pie

fruit pizza

1 package (20 ounces)
    refrigerated sliceable
    sugar cookies, sliced
1 package (8 ounces)
    PHILADELPHIA®
    Cream Cheese, softened
¼ cup sugar
½ teaspoon vanilla

Assorted fruit, such as
    sliced kiwi, strawberries,
    blueberries and drained,
    canned mandarin orange
    segments
¼ cup apricot preserves, pressed
    through sieve to remove
    lumps
1 tablespoon water

HEAT oven to 375°F. Line 12-inch pizza pan with foil; spray with cooking spray. Arrange cookie dough slices in single layer in prepared pan; press together to form crust. Bake 14 minutes; cool. Invert onto serving plate; carefully remove foil. Invert onto large serving plate or tray so crust is right-side-up.

BEAT cream cheese, sugar and vanilla with electric mixer on medium speed until well blended. Spread over crust.

ARRANGE fruit over cream cheese layer. Mix preserves and water; brush over fruit. Refrigerate 2 hours. Cut into 12 wedges to serve. Store leftover dessert in refrigerator.

Makes 12 servings (1 wedge each)

Prep Time: 25 minutes plus refrigerating

berry good sorbet

1 pint blueberries
1 package (10 ounces) frozen
    raspberries in syrup, thawed
1½ cups ginger ale

¾ cup KARO® Light Corn Syrup
    or KARO® Lite Syrup
¼ cup sugar
2 tablespoons lemon juice

1. In blender or food processor, purée blueberries and raspberries until smooth. Press through a fine-mesh strainer into a large bowl. Discard seeds.

2. Stir in ginger ale, corn syrup, sugar and lemon juice.

3. Pour into container of ice cream maker and freeze according to manufacturer's directions.

Makes about 1½ quarts

Prep Time: 15 minutes plus freezing

fruit pizza

raisin apple bread pudding

4 cups white bread cubes

1 medium apple, chopped

1 cup raisins

2 large eggs

1 can (12 fluid ounces)
NESTLÉ® CARNATION®
Evaporated Milk

½ cup apple juice

½ cup granulated sugar

1½ teaspoons ground cinnamon

1 jar caramel ice cream topping
(optional)

PREHEAT oven to 350°F. Grease 11×7-inch baking dish.

COMBINE bread, apple and raisins in large bowl. Beat eggs in medium bowl. Stir in evaporated milk, apple juice, sugar and cinnamon; mix well. Pour egg mixture over bread mixture, pressing bread into milk mixture; let stand for 10 minutes. Pour into prepared baking dish.

BAKE for 40 to 45 minutes or until set and apples are tender. Serve warm with caramel topping.

Makes 8 servings

margarita ice cream pie

1½ cups crushed pretzels

⅔ cup I CAN'T BELIEVE IT'S
NOT BUTTER!® Spread,
melted

⅓ cup sugar

1 container (1.5 quarts)
BREYERS® All Natural
Vanilla Ice Cream

1 can (6 ounces) frozen limeade
concentrate, thawed

¼ cup tequila

2 cups frozen whipped topping,
thawed

In medium bowl, combine pretzels, I Can't Believe It's Not Butter!® Spread and sugar. Press into shallow 9-inch glass pie plate sprayed with nonstick cooking spray. Freeze 10 minutes.

Meanwhile, in another medium bowl, spoon small scoops Breyers® All Natural Vanilla Ice Cream. Add limeade concentrate and tequila. With electric mixer on low speed, beat just until blended. Pour into frozen crust, pressing to form an even layer. Cover and freeze 4 hours or overnight.

Top with whipped topping and freeze an additional 30 minutes or until ready to serve. Sprinkle, if desired, with grated lime peel.

Makes 12 servings

Prep Time: 15 minutes
Freeze Time: 4 hours 40 minutes

raisin apple bread pudding

baked caramel rice custard

3 cups fat-free milk	3 eggs
½ cup **CREAM OF RICE®** Hot Cereal, uncooked	1 cup sugar, divided
1 teaspoon vanilla extract	½ teaspoon salt

1. Preheat oven to 325°F. Bring milk just to a boil in medium saucepan over medium heat. Gradually add Cream of Rice, stirring constantly. Cook and stir 1 minute longer. Remove from heat; cover. Let stand 4 minutes. Stir in vanilla.

2. Mix eggs, ⅓ cup sugar and salt until well blended. Add to Cream of Rice mixture and mix well; set aside.

3. Heat remaining ⅔ cup sugar in medium saucepan over medium heat until melted and golden brown, stirring occasionally. Immediately pour into 1½-quart baking dish, tilting dish to evenly coat bottom and sides of dish. Pour cereal mixture into prepared dish. Place in 13×9-inch baking pan; carefully add 2 cups hot water to baking pan.

4. Bake 60 to 70 minutes or until knife inserted in center comes out clean. Cool on wire rack. Unmold onto serving plate. Serve warm or chilled.   *Makes 8 servings*

Tip: To unmold the custard neatly, run a small knife around the edge of the custard. Place a serving plate over the mold and turn the mold over carefully onto the plate. Let stand at least 30 seconds or until the custard releases onto the plate.

easy southern banana pudding

3 cups cold milk	30 NILLA® Wafers
2 packages (4-serving size each) **JELL-O®** Vanilla Flavor Instant Pudding	3 medium bananas, sliced
	1 tub (8 ounces) COOL WHIP® Whipped Topping, thawed

POUR milk into large bowl. Add dry pudding mixes. Beat with wire whisk 2 minutes or until well blended. Let stand 5 minutes.

ARRANGE half of the wafers on bottom and up side of 2-quart serving bowl; top with layers of half each of the pudding and banana slices. Repeat all layers. Cover with whipped topping.

REFRIGERATE 3 hours. Store leftover dessert in refrigerator.

Makes 14 servings (about ⅔ cup each)

Healthy Living: Save 60 calories and 3.5 grams of fat per serving by preparing with fat-free milk, JELL-O® Vanilla Flavor Fat Free Sugar Free Instant Pudding, Reduced Fat NILLA® Wafers and COOL WHIP LITE® Whipped Topping.

baked caramel rice custard

chocolate mousse napoleons with strawberries & cream

½ of a 17.3-ounce package
PEPPERIDGE FARM®
Puff Pastry Sheets (1 sheet)

1 cup heavy cream

¼ teaspoon ground cinnamon

1 cup semi-sweet chocolate pieces, melted

2 cups sweetened whipped cream* or whipped topping

1½ cups sliced strawberries

1 square (1 ounce) semi-sweet chocolate, melted (optional)

Confectioners' sugar

For 2 cups sweetened whipped cream, beat 1 cup heavy cream, 2 tablespoons sugar and ¼ teaspoon vanilla extract in a chilled medium bowl with an electric mixer on high speed until stiff peaks form.

1. Thaw the pastry sheet at room temperature for 40 minutes or until it's easy to handle. Heat the oven to 400°F.

2. Unfold the pastry sheet on a lightly floured surface. Cut the pastry sheet into **3** strips along the fold marks. Cut **each** strip into **6** rectangles, making **18** pastry rectangles. Place the pastry rectangles 1 inch apart on a baking sheet.

3. Bake for 15 minutes or until the pastries are golden brown. Remove the pastries from the baking sheet and cool on a wire rack. Split **each** pastry into **2** layers, making **36** layers.

4. Beat the cream and cinnamon in a large bowl with an electric mixer on high speed until stiff peaks form. Fold in the melted chocolate pieces.

5. Spread **12** pastry layers with the chocolate cream and top with **12** pastry layers. Top with the whipped cream, strawberries and remaining pastry layers. Serve immediately or cover and refrigerate for up to 4 hours.

6. Drizzle the napoleons with the melted chocolate, if desired, and sprinkle with the confectioners' sugar just before serving.   *Makes 12 servings*

Prep Time: 1 hour 5 minutes
Bake Time: 15 minutes
Total Time: 1 hour 20 minutes

chocolate mousse napoleons with
strawberries & cream

cookies & cream freeze

4 squares BAKER'S® Semi-Sweet Baking Chocolate

14 OREO® Chocolate Sandwich Cookies, divided

1 package (8 ounces) PHILADELPHIA® Cream Cheese, softened

¼ cup sugar

½ teaspoon vanilla

1 tub (8 ounces) COOL WHIP® Whipped Topping, thawed

MELT chocolate as directed on package; set aside until ready to use. Line 8½×4½-inch loaf pan with foil, with ends of foil extending over sides of pan. Arrange 8 of the cookies evenly on bottom of pan. Crumble remaining 6 cookies; set aside.

BEAT cream cheese, sugar and vanilla in medium bowl with electric mixer until well blended. Stir in whipped topping. Remove about 1½ cups of the cream cheese mixture; place in medium bowl. Stir in melted chocolate.

SPREAD remaining cream cheese mixture over cookies in pan; sprinkle with crumbled cookies. Gently press cookies into cream cheese mixture with back of spoon; top with chocolate mixture. Cover. Freeze 3 hours or until firm. Remove from freezer about 15 minutes before serving; invert onto serving plate. Peel off foil; let stand at room temperature to soften slightly before cutting to serve.

Makes 12 servings (1 piece each)

Jazz It Up: Drizzle serving plates with additional melted BAKER'S® Semi-Sweet Chocolate for a spectacular, yet simple, dessert presentation.

Prep Time: 30 minutes plus freezing

baked apples

2 tablespoons sugar

2 tablespoons raisins, chopped

2 tablespoons chopped walnuts

2 tablespoons GRANDMA'S® Molasses

6 apples, cored

Heat oven to 350°F. In medium bowl, combine sugar, raisins, walnuts and molasses. Fill apple cavities with molasses mixture. Place in 13×9-inch baking dish. Pour ½ cup hot water over apples and bake 25 minutes or until soft. *Makes 6 servings*

cookies & cream freeze

cinnamon tacos with fruit salsa

1 cup sliced fresh strawberries
1 cup cubed fresh pineapple
1 cup cubed peeled kiwi
½ teaspoon ORTEGA® Diced Jalapeños

4 tablespoons plus 1 teaspoon granulated sugar, divided
1 tablespoon ground cinnamon
6 (8-inch) ORTEGA® Soft Flour Tortillas
Nonstick cooking spray

Stir together strawberries, pineapple, kiwi, jalapeños and 4 teaspoons sugar (adjust to taste, if desired) in large bowl; set aside.

Combine remaining 3 tablespoons sugar and cinnamon in small bowl; set aside.

Coat tortillas lightly on both sides with nonstick cooking spray. Heat each tortilla in nonstick skillet over medium heat until slightly puffed and golden brown. Remove from heat; immediately dust both sides with cinnamon-sugar mixture. Shake excess cinnamon-sugar back into bowl. Repeat cooking and dusting process until all tortillas are warmed.

Fold tortillas in half and fill with fruit mixture. Serve immediately.

Makes 6 servings

Prep Time: 20 minutes
Start to Finish Time: 30 minutes

classic minute rice pudding

3 cups milk
1 cup MINUTE® White Rice, uncooked
¼ cup sugar

¼ cup raisins
¼ teaspoon salt
2 eggs
1 teaspoon vanilla

Combine milk, rice, sugar, raisins and salt in medium saucepan. Bring to a boil, stirring constantly. Reduce heat to medium-low; simmer 6 minutes, stirring occasionally.

Beat eggs and vanilla lightly in small bowl. Stir small amount of hot mixture into eggs. Stirring constantly, slowly pour egg mixture back into hot mixture.

Cook on low heat 1 minute, stirring constantly, until thickened. DO NOT BOIL. Remove from heat. Let stand 30 minutes.

Serve warm. Store any remaining pudding in refrigerator.

Makes 4 servings

Tip: Create flavorful new varieties of rice puddings by trying different types of dried fruits instead of raisins, such as dried cherries, chopped dried apricots, chopped dried pineapple or dried sweetened cranberries.

cinnamon taco with fruit salsa

nestlé® toll house® chocolate chip pie

2 large eggs
½ cup all-purpose flour
½ cup granulated sugar
½ cup packed brown sugar
¾ cup (1½ sticks) butter, softened
1 cup (6 ounces) NESTLÉ® TOLL HOUSE® Semi-Sweet Chocolate Morsels

1 cup chopped nuts
1 *unbaked* 9-inch (4-cup volume) deep-dish pie shell*
Sweetened whipped cream or ice cream (optional)

If using frozen pie shell, use deep-dish style, thawed completely. Bake on baking sheet; increase baking time slightly.

PREHEAT oven to 325°F.

BEAT eggs in large mixer bowl on high speed until foamy. Beat in flour, granulated sugar and brown sugar. Beat in butter. Stir in morsels and nuts. Spoon into pie shell.

BAKE for 55 to 60 minutes or until knife inserted halfway between outside edge and center comes out clean. Cool on wire rack. Serve warm with whipped cream.

Makes 8 servings

raisin pear crisp

8 medium pears, quartered, cored and sliced ¼ inch thick
1 cup SUN-MAID® Raisins
½ cup granulated sugar
2 tablespoons all-purpose flour
2 tablespoons lemon juice
¾ cup packed brown sugar

¾ cup old-fashioned oats
⅔ cup all-purpose flour
1 teaspoon cinnamon
6 tablespoons butter, at room temperature
¼ cup chopped hazelnuts

HEAT oven to 350°F. Butter 13×9-inch baking dish.

GENTLY mix pears, raisins, granulated sugar, 2 tablespoons flour and lemon juice. Place in prepared dish.

COMBINE brown sugar, oats, ⅔ cup flour and cinnamon in medium bowl. With pastry blender or fingers, mix in butter until crumbly. Mix in hazelnuts.

CRUMBLE mixture over fruit.

BAKE about 40 minutes until golden brown and fruit is bubbly. Serve warm.

Makes 8 servings

Prep Time: 20 minutes
Bake Time: 40 minutes

cinnamon-spice dip

¼ cup packed brown sugar
⅛ teaspoon ground cinnamon
⅛ teaspoon ground nutmeg

2 cups thawed COOL WHIP®
Whipped Topping

STIR sugar and spices into COOL WHIP® until well blended.

REFRIGERATE 1 hour.

SERVE with strawberries, apple slices, assorted NABISCO® Cookies and HONEY MAID® Grahams Sticks.   *Makes 13 servings (about 2 tablespoons each)*

Special Extra: Garnish dip with a light sprinkling of additional cinnamon just before serving.

Prep Time: 10 minutes plus refrigerating

fresh berry-berry cobbler

¼ cup sugar
1 teaspoon cornstarch
12 ounces fresh raspberries
8 ounces fresh blueberries
¼ cup CREAM OF WHEAT®
  Hot Cereal (Instant,
  1-minute, 2½-minute
  or 10-minute cook time),
  uncooked
¼ cup all-purpose flour

¼ cup ground almonds
2 teaspoons baking powder
¼ teaspoon salt
¼ cup (½ stick) butter, cut into
  small pieces, softened
¼ cup milk
1 egg
1 tablespoon sugar
Ice cream or whipped cream
  (optional)

1. Preheat oven to 450°F. Blend sugar and cornstarch in mixing bowl. Add berries and toss to coat. Pour into 8-inch square baking pan; set aside.

2. Combine Cream of Wheat, flour, almonds, baking powder and salt in food processor. Add butter; pulse several times until well combined. Add milk and egg; pulse until mixed thoroughly. Spread evenly over fruit mixture. Sprinkle sugar over top.

3. Bake 20 minutes. Let stand 5 minutes before serving. Serve in shallow bowls with ice cream or whipped cream, if desired.   *Makes 6 servings*

Tip: For an elegant presentation, serve in a martini glass and top with a fresh sprig of mint.

Prep Time: 10 minutes
Start to Finish Time: 35 minutes

acknowledgments

The publisher would like to thank the companies and organizations listed below for the use of their recipes and photographs in this publication.

ACH Food Companies, Inc.

ARM & HAMMER®, Church & Dwight Co., Inc.

The Beef Checkoff

BelGioioso® Cheese Inc.

Bob Evans®

Cabot® Creamery Cooperative

Campbell Soup Company

Cherry Marketing Institute

Cream of Wheat® Cereal

Crystal Farms®

Delmarva Poultry Industry, Inc.

Del Monte Foods

Dole Food Company, Inc.

Domino® Foods, Inc.

Duncan Hines® and Moist Deluxe® are registered trademarks of Pinnacle Foods Corp.

Filippo Berio® Olive Oil

The Golden Grain Company®

Grandma's®, A Division of B&G Foods, Inc.

The Hershey Company

Hillshire Farm®

Hormel Foods, LLC

Jennie-O Turkey Store, LLC

Kraft Foods Global, Inc.

Lee Kum Kee®

© Mars, Incorporated 2010

McIlhenny Company (TABASCO® brand Pepper Sauce)

Mrs. Dash® SALT-FREE SEASONING BLENDS

National Honey Board

National Onion Association

Nestlé USA

Newman's Own, Inc.®

North Dakota Wheat Commission

Ortega®, A Division of B&G Foods, Inc.

Peanut Advisory Board

Polaner®, A Division of B&G Foods, Inc.

The Quaker® Oatmeal Kitchens

Reckitt Benckiser LLC.

Riviana Foods Inc.

Sargento® Foods Inc.

Sokol and Company

StarKist®

Stonyfield Farm®

Reprinted with permission of Sunkist Growers, Inc. All Rights Reserved.

Sun•Maid® Growers of California

Tyson Foods, Inc.

Unilever

USA Rice Federation®

Veg•All®

Watkins Incorporated

Wisconsin Milk Marketing Board

VOLUME MEASUREMENTS (dry)

$1/8$ teaspoon = 0.5 mL
$1/4$ teaspoon = 1 mL
$1/2$ teaspoon = 2 mL
$3/4$ teaspoon = 4 mL
1 teaspoon = 5 mL
1 tablespoon = 15 mL
2 tablespoons = 30 mL
$1/4$ cup = 60 mL
$1/3$ cup = 75 mL
$1/2$ cup = 125 mL
$2/3$ cup = 150 mL
$3/4$ cup = 175 mL
1 cup = 250 mL
2 cups = 1 pint = 500 mL
3 cups = 750 mL
4 cups = 1 quart = 1 L

VOLUME MEASUREMENTS (fluid)

1 fluid ounce (2 tablespoons) = 30 mL
4 fluid ounces ($1/2$ cup) = 125 mL
8 fluid ounces (1 cup) = 250 mL
12 fluid ounces ($1\frac{1}{2}$ cups) = 375 mL
16 fluid ounces (2 cups) = 500 mL

WEIGHTS (mass)

$1/2$ ounce = 15 g
1 ounce = 30 g
3 ounces = 90 g
4 ounces = 120 g
8 ounces = 225 g
10 ounces = 285 g
12 ounces = 360 g
16 ounces = 1 pound = 450 g

DIMENSIONS

$1/16$ inch = 2 mm
$1/8$ inch = 3 mm
$1/4$ inch = 6 mm
$1/2$ inch = 1.5 cm
$3/4$ inch = 2 cm
1 inch = 2.5 cm

OVEN TEMPERATURES

250°F = 120°C
275°F = 140°C
300°F = 150°C
325°F = 160°C
350°F = 180°C
375°F = 190°C
400°F = 200°C
425°F = 220°C
450°F = 230°C

BAKING PAN SIZES

Utensil	Size in Inches/Quarts	Metric Volume	Size in Centimeters
Baking or Cake Pan (square or rectangular)	8×8×2	2 L	20×20×5
	9×9×2	2.5 L	23×23×5
	12×8×2	3 L	30×20×5
	13×9×2	3.5 L	33×23×5
Loaf Pan	8×4×3	1.5 L	20×10×7
	9×5×3	2 L	23×13×7
Round Layer Cake Pan	8×1½	1.2 L	20×4
	9×1½	1.5 L	23×4
Pie Plate	8×1¼	750 mL	20×3
	9×1¼	1 L	23×3
Baking Dish or Casserole	1 quart	1 L	—
	1½ quart	1.5 L	—
	2 quart	2 L	—